THE COMPLETE
CREATIVE
COOK

THE COMPLETE
CREATIVE
COOK

This edition published in 1997 by
Parragon
Units 13-17
Avonbridge Trading Estate
Atlantic Road
Avonmouth
Bristol BS11 9QD

Produced by
Anness Publishing Limited
Hermes House, 88-89 Blackfriars Road
London SE1 8HA

ISBN 0-75252-154-3 (hardback)
ISBN 0-75252-165-9 (paperback)

Publisher: Joanna Lorenz
Project Editor: Carole Clements
Copy Editors: Norma MacMillan and Penny David
Designer: Sheila Volpe
Photographer: Amanda Heywood
Food Styling: Frances Cleary, Carole Handslip,
steps by Nicola Fowler

Printed and bound in Italy

ACKNOWLEDGEMENTS

For their assistance in the production of this book the publishers wish to thank:

American Country Collections Limited
28 Baker Street
Weybridge, Surrey KT13 8AU

Magimix
115A High Street
Godalming, Surrey GU7 1AQ

British Gas North Thames
North Thames House
London Road
Staines, Middlesex TW18 4AE

Prestige
Prestige House
22-26 High Street
Egham, Surrey TW20 9DU

MC Typeset Limited
The Barn, Woodbank House
Pilgrims Way
Wouldham, Kent ME1 3RB

Staks
24 The Waterglade Centre
The Broadway, Ealing
London W5 2ND

CONTENTS

~

INTRODUCTION

~

Complete creative cooking means putting together varied, tempting meals throughout the week and having friends and relatives over for dinner without stress. It used to mean rummaging through notebooks and clippings to find that special grandmother's recipe for beef stew or a neighbour's traditional chocolate cake.

In preparing this book we have brought together such favourite old recipes and also added new ideas, which reflect the increasing availability of exotic and speciality ingredients and the evolution of the way we eat. And each recipe is brought to life, every step of the way, in pictures.

It's easy to learn basic cooking know-how with the help of this book. With pictures to guide you at every stage, even a beginner can cook meals with confidence. For the experienced cook, the step-by-step photographs serve as memory joggers. You will practically be able to cook at a glance from a treasury of over 200 recipes.

To start off a meal or sit down to a simple one, there are chunky soups and cold ones, plus sandwiches to eat with both hands, and appetizers both plain and fancy. The seafood recipes take full advantage of the increasingly wide variety of fish and shellfish available locally. For many people, meat and poultry are the heart of a meal, and the choice here includes long-simmering as well as speedy dishes. An increasing trend towards grains and fresh produce is reflected here, with recipes for pasta, pizza, beans and vegetables well represented. Time set aside for baking may seem a luxury these days, but with the steps simply laid out, it requires only a small amount of effort to fill the kitchen with mouth-watering smells.

Here is creative family cooking in all its variety. In the category of snug, winter night's fare we have chosen such standbys as macaroni cheese, traditional chicken potpie and peach cobbler. Sometimes we put a twist on the basics, offering baby chickens with cranberry sauce, cheeseburgers with spicy avocado relish, and hazelnut sundaes with hot fudge sauce. International dishes are also given fair showing, with Mexican chicken, jambalaya, pork with sauerkraut and Spanish omelette just some of the favourites to be found here.

The only thing that's missing in *The Complete Creative Cook* are the aromas. Still, there's no substitute for experience. Only you know the quirks of your oven and how to get the best from your utensils. Setting out all the ingredients before beginning is just sound culinary practice. Even perfect technique won't remedy a lack of flavour, so good ingredients are essential to good cooking. Stay in tune with the seasons, choosing fruits and vegetables at their peak. And remember to taste and adjust the seasoning, if necessary, before serving.

Our hectic schedules leave us less time in the kitchen these days, but we hope this book rekindles the pleasures of family cooking. Homemade food will make a comeback in your house with the help of *The Complete Creative Cook*.

SOUPS, SANDWICHES
& APPETIZERS

~

Here you will find soups hot and cold, for winter and summer; mouthwatering sandwiches, and a wealth of appetizing finger-food for first courses.

Warming Winter Vegetable Soup

SERVES 8

1 medium-size head of Savoy cabbage, quartered and cored

2 tbsp vegetable oil

4 carrots, thinly sliced

2 celery sticks, thinly sliced

2 parsnips, diced

2½ pt (1.5 litres) chicken stock

3 medium-size potatoes, diced

2 courgettes, sliced

1 small red pepper, seeded and diced

1 small cauliflower, stems trimmed and separated into florets

2 tomatoes, seeded and diced

½ tsp fresh thyme leaves, or ¼ tsp dried thyme

2 tbsp chopped fresh parsley

salt and pepper

1 Slice the cabbage quarters into thin strips across the leaves.

2 ▲ Heat the oil in a large saucepan. Add the cabbage, carrots, celery and parsnips and cook 10–15 minutes over medium heat, stirring frequently.

3 Stir the stock into the vegetables and bring to the boil. Skim off any foam that rises to the top.

4 ▲ Add the potatoes, courgettes, pepper, cauliflower and tomatoes with the herbs, and salt and pepper to taste. Bring back to the boil. Reduce the heat to low, cover the pan, and simmer until the vegetables are tender, 15–20 minutes.

Traditional Tomato Soup

SERVES 4

1 oz (30 g) butter or margarine

1 onion, chopped

2 lb (900 g) tomatoes, quartered

2 carrots, chopped

16 fl oz (500 ml) chicken stock

2 tbsp chopped fresh parsley

½ tsp fresh thyme leaves, or ¼ tsp dried thyme

3 fl oz (85 ml) whipping cream (optional)

salt and pepper

1 Melt the butter or margarine in a large saucepan. Add the onion and cook until softened, about 5 minutes.

2 ▲ Stir in the tomatoes, carrots, chicken stock, parsley and thyme. Bring to the boil. Reduce the heat to low, cover the pan, and simmer until tender, 15–20 minutes.

3 ▼ Purée the soup in a vegetable mill. Return the puréed soup to the saucepan.

4 Stir in the cream, if using, and reheat gently. Season with salt and pepper. Ladle into warmed soup bowls and serve hot, sprinkled with a little more thyme, if you wish.

~ COOK'S TIP ~

Canned Italian plum tomatoes are ideal for this soup.

Warming Winter Vegetable Soup (top), Traditional Tomato Soup

Carrot Soup

SERVES 6

1 oz (30 g) butter or margarine

1 onion, chopped

1 celery stick, chopped

1 medium-sized potato, chopped

1½ lb (700 g) carrots, chopped

2 tsp grated fresh root ginger

2 pt (1.25 litres) chicken stock

3 fl oz (85 ml) whipping cream

¼ teaspoon grated nutmeg

salt and pepper

1 ▼ Combine the butter or margarine, onion and celery and cook until softened, about 5 minutes.

2 Stir in the potato, carrots, ginger and stock. Bring to the boil. Reduce the heat to low, cover the pan and simmer 20 minutes.

3 ▲ Pour the soup into a food processor or blender and process until smooth. Alternatively, use a vegetable mill to purée the soup. Return the soup to the pan. Stir in the cream and nutmeg and add salt and pepper to taste. Reheat gently for serving.

Minty Pea Soup

SERVES 6

1 oz (30 g) butter or margarine

1 onion, chopped

1 small head of lettuce, shredded

2 lb (900 g) shelled fresh green peas or frozen peas, thawed

2½ pt (1.5 litres) chicken stock

3 tbsp chopped fresh mint

salt and pepper

6 fl oz (175 ml) whipping cream

fresh mint sprigs, for garnishing

~ VARIATION ~

To serve cold, refrigerate the puréed soup until thoroughly chilled, 3–4 hours. Stir all the cream into the soup just before serving, or keep some to swirl over each serving.

1 ▲ Melt the butter or margarine in a large saucepan. Add the onion and cook until softened, about 5 minutes.

2 ▲ Stir in the lettuce, peas, stock and mint. Bring to the boil. Reduce the heat to low, cover the pan and simmer 15 minutes.

3 Pour the soup into a blender or food processor and process until smooth. Alternatively, purée the soup in a vegetable mill. Return the puréed soup to the pan. Season to taste.

4 ▲ Stir in two-thirds of the cream and reheat gently. Ladle into bowls and serve with the remaining cream. For a decorative effect, pour a scant tablespoon of cream in a spiral design into the centre of each serving, or stir it in and garnish with sprigs of mint.

Carrot Soup (top), Minty Pea Soup

Chilled Avocado and Courgette Soup

SERVES 6

1¾ pt (1 litre) chicken stock

1 lb (450 g) courgettes, sliced

2 large, very ripe avocados

3 tbsp fresh lemon juice

6 fl oz (175 ml) plain yogurt

2 tsp Worcestershire sauce

½ tsp chilli powder

⅛ tsp sugar

dash of chilli sauce

salt

1 In a large saucepan, bring the chicken stock to the boil.

2 ▲ Add the courgettes and simmer until soft, 10–15 minutes. Let cool.

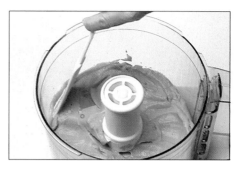

3 ▲ Peel the avocados. Remove and discard the stones. Cut the flesh into chunks and put in a food processor or blender. Add the lemon juice and process until smooth.

4 ▲ Using a slotted spoon, transfer the courgettes to the food processor or blender; reserve the stock. Process the courgettes with the avocado purée.

5 ▲ Pour the avocado-courgette purée into a bowl. Stir in the reserved stock. Add two-thirds of the yogurt, the Worcestershire sauce, chilli powder, sugar, chilli sauce and salt to taste. Mix well. Cover tightly and chill 3–4 hours.

6 To serve, ladle the soup into bowls. Swirl the remaining yogurt on the surface.

Chicken Soup with Noodles

SERVES 8

1 × 3 lb (1.35 kg) chicken, cut in pieces
2 onions, quartered
1 parsnip, quartered
2 carrots, quartered
½ tsp salt
1 bay leaf
2 allspice berries
4 black peppercorns
4¾ pt (3 litres) water
3 oz (85 g) very thin egg noodles
sprigs of fresh dill, for garnishing

1 ▲ In a large saucepan, combine the chicken pieces, onions, parsnip, carrots, salt, bay leaf, allspice berries and peppercorns.

2 ▲ Add the water to the pan and bring to the boil, skimming frequently.

3 Reduce the heat to low and simmer 1½ hours, skimming occasionally.

4 Strain the broth through a fine-mesh strainer into a bowl. Cool then refrigerate overnight.

5 ▲ When the chicken pieces are cool enough to handle, remove the meat from the bones. Discard the bones, skin, vegetables and flavourings. Chop the chicken meat and refrigerate overnight.

6 Remove the solidified fat from the surface of the chilled broth. Pour the broth into a saucepan and bring to the boil. Taste the broth; if a more concentrated flavour is wanted, boil 10 minutes to reduce slightly.

7 ▲ Add the chicken meat and noodles to the broth and cook until the noodles are tender, about 8 minutes (check packet instructions for timing). Serve hot, garnished with dill sprigs.

Green Bean Soup with Parmesan Cheese

SERVES 4

1 oz (30 g) butter or margarine

8 oz (225 g) green beans, trimmed

1 garlic clove, crushed

16 fl oz (500 ml) vegetable stock

salt and pepper

2 oz (55 g) Parmesan cheese

2 fl oz (65 ml) single cream

2 tbsp chopped fresh parsley

1 Melt the butter or margarine in a medium saucepan. Add the green beans and garlic and cook 2–3 minutes over medium heat, stirring frequently.

2 ▲ Stir in the stock and season with salt and pepper. Bring to the boil. Reduce the heat and simmer, uncovered, until the beans are tender, 10–15 minutes.

3 ▼ Pour the soup into a blender or food processor and process until smooth. Alternatively, purée the soup in a food mill. Return to the pan. Stir in the grated cheese and cream. Sprinkle with the parsley and serve.

Hearty Lentil Soup

SERVES 6

6 oz (175 g) brown lentils

1¾ pt (1 litre) chicken stock

8 fl oz (250 ml) water

2 fl oz (65 ml) dry red wine

1½ lb (700 g) ripe tomatoes, peeled, seeded and chopped, or 14 oz (400 g) canned chopped tomatoes

1 carrot, sliced

1 onion, chopped

1 celery stick, sliced

1 garlic clove, crushed

¼ tsp ground coriander

2 tsp chopped fresh basil, or ½ tsp dried basil

1 bay leaf

6 tbsp freshly grated Parmesan cheese

1 ▲ Rinse the lentils and discard any discoloured ones and any grit.

2 ▲ Combine the lentils, stock, water, wine, tomatoes, carrot, onion, celery and garlic in a large saucepan. Add the coriander, basil and bay leaf.

3 ▼ Bring to the boil, reduce the heat to low, cover and simmer until the lentils are just tender, 20–25 minutes, stirring occasionally.

4 Discard the bay leaf. Ladle the soup into 6 soup bowls and sprinkle each with 1 tablespoon of the cheese.

> ~ **VARIATION** ~
>
> For a more substantial soup, add about 4 oz (115 g) finely chopped cooked ham for the last 10 minutes of cooking.

Green Bean Soup with Parmesan Cheese (top), Hearty Lentil Soup

Spicy Mixed Bean Soup

SERVES 8

12 oz (350 g) dried black or red kidney beans, soaked overnight

3½ pt (2 litres) water

6 garlic cloves, crushed

12 oz (350 g) dried haricot or white beans, soaked overnight

6 tbsp balsamic or white wine vinegar

4 chilli peppers, seeded and chopped

6 spring onions, finely chopped

juice of 1 lime or lemon

2 fl oz (65 ml) olive oil

3 tbsp chopped fresh coriander, plus more for garnishing

salt and pepper

1 Drain and rinse the black or red kidney beans. Place them in a large saucepan with half the water and garlic. Bring to the boil. Reduce the heat to low, cover and simmer until the beans are soft, about 1½ hours.

2 Drain and rinse the white beans. Put them in another saucepan with the remaining water and garlic. Bring to a boil, cover and simmer until soft, about 1 hour.

3 ▲ Purée the cooked haricot or white beans in a food processor or blender. Stir in the vinegar, chilli peppers and half the spring onions. Return to the saucepan and reheat gently.

4 Purée the other cooked beans. Return to the saucepan and stir in the lime or lemon juice, olive oil, coriander and the remaining spring onions. Reheat gently.

5 ▲ Season both soups with salt and pepper. To serve, place a ladleful of each puréed soup in each soup bowl, side by side. Swirl the two soups together with a cocktail stick. If liked, garnish with extra chopped fresh coriander.

Warming Autumn Soup

SERVES 4

1 oz (30 g) butter or margarine

2 small onions, finely chopped

1 lb (450 g) butternut squash or pumpkin, peeled, seeded and cubed

2 pt (1.25 litres) chicken stock

8 oz (225 g) potatoes, cubed

1 tsp paprika

4 fl oz (125 ml) whipping cream (optional)

salt and pepper

1½ tbsp chopped fresh chives, plus whole chives, for garnishing

1 Melt the butter or margarine in a large saucepan. Add the onions and cook until soft, about 5 minutes.

2 ▲ Add the squash or pumpkin, stock, potatoes and paprika. Bring to the boil. Reduce the heat to low, cover the pan and simmer until the vegetables are soft, about 35 minutes.

3 Pour the soup into a food processor or blender and process until smooth. Return the soup to the pan and stir in the cream, if using. Season with salt and pepper. Reheat gently.

4 ▲ Stir in the chopped chives just before serving. If liked, garnish each serving with a few whole chives.

Spicy Mixed Bean Soup (top), Warming Autumn Soup

Mozzarella Cheese and Tomato Sandwiches

SERVES 4

4 small round white bread rolls

4 fl oz (125 ml) freshly made or bottled pesto sauce

8 oz (225 g) Mozzarella cheese, thinly sliced

4 medium tomatoes, thinly sliced

3 tbsp olive oil

fresh basil leaves, for garnishing

1 With a serrated knife, cut each roll open in half. Spread 1 tablespoon of pesto sauce over the cut side of each half.

2 ▲ Arrange alternating slices of Mozzarella cheese and tomato on the bottom half of each roll.

3 ▲ Drizzle the olive oil over the cheese and tomatoes.

4 Replace the top half of each roll; garnish with basil leaves, if you wish.

Greek Salad in Pitta Bread

SERVES 6

½ small head of iceberg lettuce, cut in fine strips across the leaves

½ cucumber, diced

9 cherry tomatoes, halved

2 spring onions, finely chopped

4 oz (115 g) feta cheese, crumbled

8 black olives, stoned and chopped

6 oval pitta breads, cut in half crosswise

FOR THE DRESSING

1 small garlic clove, crushed

⅛ tsp salt

1 tsp fresh lemon juice

2 tbsp olive oil

1 tsp chopped fresh mint

pepper

1 ▲ In a bowl, combine the lettuce, cucumber, tomatoes, spring onions, feta cheese and olives.

2 ▲ For the dressing, combine all the ingredients in a small screwtop jar and shake well to mix.

3 ▲ Pour the dressing over the salad and toss together.

4 ▲ Gently open the pitta bread halves. Fill the pockets with the salad. Serve immediately.

Mozzarella Cheese and Tomato Sandwiches (top), Greek Salad in Pitta Bread

Club Sandwiches

SERVES 4

8 rashers of bacon

12 slices of white bread, toasted

4 fl oz (125 ml) mayonnaise

4–8 oz (115–225 g) cooked chicken breast meat, sliced

8 large lettuce leaves

salt and pepper

1 beef tomato, cut across in 4 slices

1 ▼ In a heavy frying pan, fry the bacon until crisp and the fat is rendered. Drain on kitchen paper.

2 Lay 4 slices of toast on a flat surface. Spread them with some of the mayonnaise.

3 ▲ Top each slice with one-quarter of the chicken and a lettuce leaf. Season with salt and pepper.

4 ▲ Spread 4 of the remaining toast slices with mayonnaise. Lay them on top of the lettuce.

5 ▲ Top each sandwich with a slice of tomato, 2 rashers of bacon and another lettuce leaf.

6 Spread the remaining slices of toast with the rest of the mayonnaise. Place them on top of the sandwiches, mayonnaise-side down.

7 Cut each sandwich into 4 triangles and secure each triangle with a cocktail stick.

Chilli Hot Dogs

Serves 6

6 frankfurters

6 large finger rolls, split open

1 oz (30 g) butter or margarine

1½ oz (45 g) Cheddar cheese, grated

1½ oz (45 g) red onion, chopped

For the chilli

2 tbsp corn oil

1 small onion, chopped

½ green pepper, seeded and chopped

8 oz (225 g) minced beef

8 fl oz (250 ml) fresh tomatoes, blanched, skinned, cooked and sieved

3 oz (85 g) drained canned red kidney beans

2 tsp chilli powder, or to taste

salt and pepper

3 ▼ Stir in the sieved tomatoes, beans, chilli powder and salt and pepper to taste. Cover the pan and simmer 10 minutes.

4 Meanwhile, put the frankfurters in a saucepan and cover with cold water. Bring to the boil. Remove from the heat, cover and let stand 5 minutes.

5 ▲ Spread both sides of each finger roll with the butter or margarine. Fry in a hot frying pan until golden brown on both sides.

6 To serve, put a frankfurter in each bun. Top with chilli and sprinkle with cheese and onion. Serve immediately.

1 ▲ For the chilli, heat the oil in a frying pan. Add the onion and green pepper and cook until softened, about 5 minutes.

2 ▲ Add the beef and cook until well browned, stirring frequently and breaking up lumps with the side of a wooden spatula.

Fried Cheddar and Chutney Sandwiches

SERVES 4

1½ oz (45 g) butter or margarine

3 large garlic cloves, crushed

3 fl oz (85 ml) homemade or bottled
  mango chutney

8 slices of white bread

8 oz (225 g) Cheddar cheese, grated

1 ▲ Melt the butter or margarine in a small saucepan. Add the garlic and cook until softened but not brown, about 2 minutes, stirring. Remove from the heat.

2 ▲ Spread the chutney on 4 slices of bread.

3 ▲ Divide the cheese among the 4 bread slices, spreading it evenly. Top with the remaining bread slices.

4 ▲ Brush both sides of each sandwich with the garlic butter.

5 Fry the sandwiches in a hot frying pan over a medium heat until golden brown, about 2 minutes on each side. Serve immediately.

~ **COOK'S TIP** ~

Well-aged mature cheddar cheese works best in combination with the strong flavours of the chutney and garlic.

Tuna and Tomato Rolls

SERVES 4

2 × 7 oz (200 g) cans tuna fish, drained

2 tbsp finely chopped black olives

2 fl oz (65 ml) finely chopped drained
  sun-dried tomatoes preserved in oil

3 spring onions, finely chopped

4 round white bread rolls, split open

1 handful rocket or small lettuce leaves

FOR THE DRESSING

1½ tbsp red wine vinegar

5 tbsp olive oil

3 tbsp chopped fresh basil

salt and pepper

1 ▼ For the dressing, combine the vinegar and oil in a mixing bowl. Whisk until an emulsion is formed. Stir in the basil. Season with salt and pepper.

2 Add the tuna, olives, sun-dried tomatoes and spring onions and stir.

3 ▲ Divide the tuna mixture among the rolls. Top with the rocket or lettuce leaves and replace the tops of the rolls, pressing them on firmly.

Fried Cheddar and Chutney Sandwiches (top), Tuna and Tomato Rolls

Roast Beef and Horseradish Open Sandwiches

SERVES 4

4 slices of pumpernickel or rye bread

12 oz (350 g) roast beef, thinly sliced

salt and pepper

4 tbsp mayonnaise

1½ tbsp prepared horseradish

2 small tomatoes, seeded and chopped

2–2 tbsp finely chopped pickled gherkin

fresh dill sprigs, for garnishing

1 ▲ Lay the slices of pumpernickel or rye bread on a flat surface. Divide the slices of roast beef between the bread, folding the slices in half, if large. Season with salt and pepper.

2 In a small bowl, combine the mayonnaise and horseradish. Stir in the tomatoes and pickled gherkin.

3 ▲ Spoon the horseradish mayonnaise onto the beef. Garnish with dill sprigs and serve.

Roast Pork and Coleslaw Rolls

SERVES 6

6 fl oz (175 ml) mayonnaise

2 tbsp tomato ketchup

¼–½ tsp cayenne pepper

1 tbsp light brown sugar

1 lb (450 g) roast pork, thinly sliced

1 lb (450 g) green or white cabbage, cut into wedges

2 carrots, finely grated

1 small green pepper, seeded and diced

½ small red onion, finely chopped

12 small round white bread rolls, split open

~ **VARIATIONS** ~

Instead of roast pork, substitute cooked ham or turkey, and prepare as above. As an alternative, try tuna in place of meat.

1 ▲ In a bowl, combine the mayonnaise, ketchup, cayenne and brown sugar. Stir well.

2 Stack the slices of roast pork. With a sharp knife, cut them into matchstick strips.

3 Remove the cores from the cabbage wedges. Lay them on a chopping board and cut into fine strips across the leaves.

4 ▲ Add the pork, cabbage, carrots, green pepper and red onion to the mayonnaise mixture. Toss to mix.

5 ▲ Fill the split bread rolls with the pork and coleslaw mixure.

Roast Beef and Horseradish Open Sandwiches (top), Roast Pork and Coleslaw Rolls

Baked Potatoes with Cheesy Topping

MAKES 20

20 small new potatoes

2 fl oz (65 ml) vegetable oil

coarse salt

4 fl oz (125 ml) soured cream

1 oz (30 g) blue cheese, crumbled

2 tbsp chopped fresh chives

1 Preheat a 350°F/180°C/Gas 4 oven.

2 Wash and dry the potatoes. Pour the oil into a bowl. Add the potatoes and toss to coat well with oil.

3 ▼ Dip the potatoes in the coarse salt to coat lightly. Spread out the potatoes on a baking sheet. Bake until tender, 45–50 minutes.

4 ▲ In a small bowl, combine the soured cream and blue cheese.

5 ▲ Cut a cross in the top of each potato. Press with your fingers to open the potatoes.

6 ▲ Top each potato with a dollop of the cheese mixture. Sprinkle with chives and serve immediately.

Avocado Dip with Spicy Tortilla Chips

SERVES 10

2 very ripe avocados
2 shallots or spring onions, chopped
2 tbsp fresh lime juice
1 tsp salt
2 tsp chilli powder
1 medium-size tomato, seeded and chopped
FOR THE TORTILLA CHIPS
3 tbsp corn oil
1½ tsp ground cumin
1 tsp salt
9 × 6 in (15 cm) corn tortillas, each cut in 6 triangles

1 Preheat a 300°F/150°C/Gas 2 oven.

2 ▲ For the tortilla chips, combine the oil, cumin and salt in a bowl.

3 ▲ Spread the tortilla triangles on 2 baking sheets. Brush the seasoned oil on both sides. Bake until they are crisp and golden, about 20 minutes, turning once or twice and brushing with the seasoned oil. Let cool.

4 ▼ Peel the avocados, discard the stones, and chop the flesh. In a food processor or blender, combine the avocados, shallots or spring onions, lime juice, salt and chilli powder. Process until smooth.

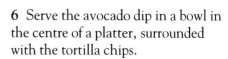

5 ▲ Transfer the mixture to a bowl. Gently stir in the chopped tomato.

6 Serve the avocado dip in a bowl in the centre of a platter, surrounded with the tortilla chips.

Pancakes with Soured Cream and Salmon

MAKES 25

8 oz (225 g) salmon fillet, skinned
juice of 1 lime or lemon
2 fl oz (65 ml) extra-virgin olive oil
pinch salt
3 tbsp chopped fresh dill
5 fl oz (150 ml) soured cream
¼ avocado, peeled and diced
3 tbsp chopped fresh chives
fresh dill sprigs, for garnishing
FOR THE PANCAKES
3 oz (85 g) buckwheat flour
2 tsp caster sugar
1 egg
4 fl oz (125 ml) milk
1 oz (30 g) butter or margarine, melted
½ tsp cream of tartar
¼ tsp bicarbonate of soda
1 tbsp water

1 ▲ With a long, sharp knife, slice the salmon as thinly as possible. Place the slices, in one layer, in a large non-metallic dish.

~ COOK'S TIP ~

For easy entertaining, make the pancakes early in the day and store, covered. To serve, arrange them on a baking tray, and reheat in a preheated 400°F/200°C/Gas 6 oven until hot, 3–4 minutes.

2 ▲ In a small bowl, combine the lime juice, olive oil, salt and chopped dill. Pour the mixture over the salmon. Cover tightly and refrigerate several hours or overnight.

3 ▲ For the pancakes, combine the buckwheat flour and sugar in a mixing bowl. Set aside.

4 ▲ In a small bowl, beat together the egg, milk and butter or margarine. Gradually stir the egg mixture into the flour mixture. Stir in the cream of tartar, bicarbonate of soda and water.

5 ▲ Cover the bowl and let the batter stand 1 hour.

6 With a sharp knife, cut the marinated salmon in thin strips.

7 ▲ To cook the pancakes, heat a heavy non-stick frying pan. Using a large spoon, drop the batter into the pan to make small pancakes about 2 in (5 cm) in diameter. When bubbles appear on the surface, turn over. Cook until the other side is golden brown, 1–2 minutes longer. Transfer the pancakes to a plate and continue until all the batter is used.

8 ▲ To serve, place a teaspoon of soured cream on each pancake and top with the marinated salmon. Sprinkle with the diced avocado and chives and garnish with dill sprigs.

Smoked Salmon Buns

MAKES 25

2 oz (55 g) cornmeal or polenta
1 oz (30 g) plain flour
½ tsp baking powder
⅛ tsp salt
1 tbsp sugar
1 egg
4 fl oz (125 ml) buttermilk
2 fl oz (65 ml) single cream
2½ oz (70 g) smoked salmon, cut in fine strips

1 Preheat a 400°F/200°C/Gas 6 oven. Grease 1–2 small bun trays.

2 In a mixing bowl, combine the cornmeal, flour, baking powder, salt and sugar. Set aside.

3 ▼ In another bowl, mix together the egg, buttermilk and cream. Gradually add the egg mixture to the cornmeal mixture, stirring quickly until just combined.

4 ▲ Stir the smoked salmon strips into the bun mixture.

5 Fill the small bun trays three-quarters full with the bun mixture. Bake until slightly risen and golden brown, 18–20 minutes. Let cool 5 minutes in the trays on a wire rack before unmoulding.

Spicy Mexican Snack Cups

MAKES 30

14 oz (400 g) canned black or red kidney beans, rinsed and drained
2 tomatoes, seeded and diced
1 garlic clove, crushed
1 shallot or ½ small onion, minced
1 chilli pepper, seeded and chopped
1 tsp finely grated lime or lemon rind
1 tbsp olive oil
2 tbsp fresh lime or lemon juice
2 tsp maple syrup
salt and pepper
3 tbsp chopped fresh coriander
FOR THE CUPS
10 × 6 in (15 cm) corn tortillas
3–4 tbsp corn oil, for brushing

1 Preheat a 400°F/200°C/Gas 6 oven.

2 ▼ For the cups, using a 2 in (5 cm) round pastry cutter, cut 3 rounds from each tortilla, pressing firmly to cut through. Discard the tortilla trimmings. Brush both sides of each tortilla round with oil.

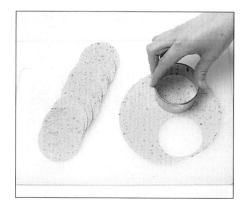

3 Press the tortilla rounds into small bun trays. Bake until crisp, about 6 minutes. Let cool on a wire rack.

4 ▲ In a mixing bowl, combine the beans, tomatoes, garlic, shallot or onion, chilli pepper, lime rind, oil, lime juice and maple syrup. Stir in salt and pepper to taste.

5 Place a spoonful of the bean and tomato mixture in each cup. Sprinkle with the chopped coriander just before serving.

Smoked Salmon Buns (top), Spicy Mexican Snack Cups

Cheesy Twists with Fruit Sauce

MAKES 12

6 large sheets of frozen filo pastry,
    thawed

4 oz (115 g) butter or margarine, melted

8 oz (225 g) Brie cheese, finely diced

FOR THE SAUCE

3 oz (85 g) cranberries or redcurrants

2 tbsp light brown sugar

1 For the sauce, combine the cranberries or redcurrants and sugar in a small saucepan with just enough water to cover. Bring to the boil and simmer until the fruit 'pop', about 3 minutes, stirring.

2 ▼ Pour the fruit mixture into a blender or food processor and process until finely chopped. Press it through a fine-mesh nylon sieve into a bowl. Taste and add more sugar if needed. Set aside.

3 Preheat a 450°F/230°C/Gas 8 oven.

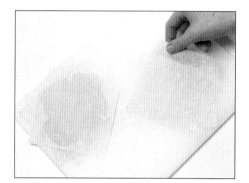

4 ▲ To make the cheesy twists, cut the filo pastry into 36 × 5 in (13 cm) squares. Lay one pastry square on a flat surface and brush with some of the butter or margarine. Lay a second pastry square on top, placing it so the corners are not on top of each other. Brush with butter. Lay a third pastry square on top, again placing it so the corners are not on top of the others, thus forming a 12-pointed star.

5 Put a heaped tablespoon of the diced cheese in the centre of each pastry star.

6 ▲ Bring the points of each pastry star up over the cheese and twist to close securely. Fold back the tips of the points.

7 Arrange the twists on a baking tray. Bake until the pastry is crisp and golden brown, 10–15 minutes.

8 Meanwhile, gently reheat the fruit sauce. Serve the cheese twists hot with the sauce.

Spicy Bean Snacks

SERVES 8

2 tbsp vegetable oil
2 onions, chopped
2 garlic cloves, chopped
3 chilli peppers, seeded and chopped
1½ tbsp mild chilli powder
1 × 16 oz (450 g) can red kidney beans, drained and liquid reserved
3 tbsp chopped fresh coriander
nacho chips (fried tortilla rounds) or tortilla chips, for serving
8 oz (225 g) Cheddar cheese, grated
3 oz (85 g) stoned black olives, thinly sliced
fresh coriander sprigs, for garnishing

1 Preheat a 425°F/220°C/Gas 7 oven.

2 ▼ Heat the oil in a frying pan. Add the onions, garlic and chilli peppers and cook until soft, about 5 minutes. Add the chilli powder and cook 1 minute more.

~ **VARIATION** ~

To serve as a bean dip, stir in the cheese and olives. Transfer the bean mixture to a round earthenware dish. Bake until the cheese melts and browns slightly, 10–15 minutes. Garnish with coriander, and serve with tortilla chips for dipping.

3 ▲ Stir the beans into the onion mixture with 4 fl oz (125 ml) of the reserved can liquid. Cook until thickened, about 10 minutes, mashing the beans with a fork from time to time. Remove the pan from the heat and stir in the chopped coriander.

4 ▼ Put a little of the bean mixture on each nacho chip. Top each nacho with a little cheese and a slice of olive. Arrange on a baking tray.

5 Bake until the cheese has melted and is beginning to brown, 5–10 minutes. Serve immediately. Garnish with coriander, if liked.

Cheese and Spinach Pastry Delights

SERVES 20

2 tbsp olive oil
2 shallots or 1 small onion, finely chopped
1 lb (450 g) frozen spinach, thawed
4 oz (115 g) feta cheese, crumbled
2 oz (55 g) chopped walnuts
¼ tsp grated nutmeg
salt and pepper
4 large sheets frozen filo pastry, thawed
4 oz (115 g) butter or margarine, melted

1 Preheat a 400°F/200°C/Gas 6 oven.

2 ▲ Heat the olive oil in a frying pan. Add the shallots or onion and cook until softened, about 5 minutes.

3 ▲ A handful at a time, squeeze all the liquid out of the spinach. Add the spinach to the shallots or onion. Increase the heat to high and cook, stirring, until all excess moisture has evaporated, about 5 minutes.

4 ▲ Transfer the spinach mixture to a bowl. Let cool. Stir in the feta and walnuts. Season with nutmeg, salt and pepper.

5 ▲ Lay a filo sheet on a flat surface. (Keep the remaining filo covered with a damp tea towel to prevent it drying out.) Brush with some of the butter or margarine. Lay a second filo sheet on top of the first. With scissors, cut the layered filo pastry lengthwise into 3 in (8 cm) wide strips.

~ VARIATION ~

For an alternative filling, omit the spinach and shallots. Use 12 oz (350 g) crumbled goat cheese, instead of the feta cheese, and 2 oz (55 g) toasted pine kernels instead of the walnuts. Mix the cheese with the olive oil and 1 tablespoon chopped fresh basil.

6 ▲ Place a tablespoonful of the spinach mixture at the end of one strip of filo pastry.

7 ▲ Fold a bottom corner of the pastry over the filling to form a triangle, then continue folding over the pastry strip to the other end. Fill and shape the triangles until all the ingredients are used.

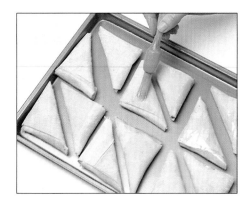

8 ▲ Set the triangles on baking sheets and brush with butter. Bake the filo triangles until they are crispy and golden brown, about 10 minutes. Serve hot.

Potato Pancakes with a Tangy Dip

MAKES 40

2 tbsp butter or margarine

1 shallot, finely chopped

1 egg

8 oz (225 g) potatoes

salt and pepper

oil for frying

FOR THE DIP

4 oz (115 g) cream cheese

2 tbsp soured cream

1 tsp finely grated lemon rind

1 tbsp fresh lemon juice

1 tbsp chopped fresh chives

1 Melt the butter or margarine in a small frying pan. Add the shallot and cook until softened, about 3 minutes. Set aside and let cool.

2 Beat the egg in a large mixing bowl until light and frothy.

3 Coarsely grate the potatoes. Add them to the bowl and mix with the egg until completely coated. Season generously with salt and pepper. Add the shallot and mix well.

4 ▼ For the tangy dip, combine the cream cheese and soured cream in a bowl. Beat until smooth. Add the lemon rind and juice and the chives. Set aside.

5 ▲ Heat ¼ in (5 mm) of oil in a frying pan. Drop teaspoonfuls of the potato mixture into the hot oil and press them with the back of a spoon to make flat rounds. Fry until well browned, 2–3 minutes on each side. Drain on kitchen paper and keep warm. Fry the remaining pancakes.

6 Serve the pancakes hot, with the dip either spooned on top or served in a separate bowl.

Cherry Tomatoes Stuffed with Crab

MAKES 40

4 oz (115 g) crab meat

1 tsp chilli sauce

¼ tsp Dijon mustard

2 tbsp mayonnaise

½ tsp Worcestershire sauce

2 spring onions, finely chopped

1 tbsp chopped fresh basil

1 tbsp chopped fresh chives

40 cherry tomatoes

salt

1 In a mixing bowl, combine the crab meat, chilli sauce, mustard, mayonnaise, Worcestershire sauce, spring onions and herbs. Mix well. Cover and refrigerate until needed.

2 ▲ Using a serrated knife, cut a very thin slice from the stem end of each tomato. Carefully scoop out the pulp and seeds with the tip of a teaspoon.

3 Sprinkle the insides of the tomato shells lightly with salt. Invert them on kitchen paper and let them drain 15 minutes.

4 ▲ Using a small spoon, stuff the tomatoes with the crab, mounding the filling slightly on top. Serve cold.

Potato Pancakes with a Tangy Dip (top), Cherry Tomatoes Stuffed with Crab

FISH & SEAFOOD

~

Whether fresh from the sea, or frozen or canned, fish and
seafood make nutritious and easy-to-prepare dishes. The
recipes here offer exciting ideas, from rich stews and stir-fries
to tasty kebabs and grilled steaks.

Fish with Orange and Caper Sauce

SERVES 4

2 fl oz (65 ml) fresh orange juice

1 tsp soy sauce

2 tbsp olive oil

4 × 8 oz (225 g) swordfish or other firm, white fish steaks

salt and pepper

1½ oz (45 g) cold butter or margarine, cut into pieces

2 tbsp capers in vinegar

1 tbsp chopped fresh parsley

1 In a small bowl, combine the orange juice, soy sauce and 1 tablespoon of the olive oil. Whisk to mix.

2 Lay the fish steaks in a shallow baking dish. Pour the orange-soy mixture over them and sprinkle with salt and pepper.

3 Heat the remaining tablespoon of olive oil in a heavy frying pan over a medium-high heat.

4 ▲ Drain the fish steaks, reserving the marinade. Add the steaks to the frying pan and cook until the fish flakes easily when tested with a fork, 3–4 minutes on each side, basting occasionally with the reserved marinade. Transfer the fish steaks to a warmed serving platter.

5 ▲ Pour the reserved marinade into the pan and cook 1 minute, stirring to mix in the cooking juices. Add the butter or margarine, capers with their vinegar, and parsley. Cook until the butter has melted and the sauce is slightly syrupy.

6 Pour the sauce over the fish steaks and serve immediately.

Tuna with Oriental Dressing

SERVES 6

6 tuna steaks (about 2 lb/900 g)

FOR THE DRESSING

1 in (2.5 cm) piece of fresh root ginger, peeled and finely grated

2 spring onions, thinly sliced

2 tbsp chopped fresh chives

grated rind and juice of 1 lime or lemon

2 tbsp dry sherry

1 tbsp soy sauce

4 fl oz (125 ml) olive oil

salt and pepper

1 ▲ For the dressing, combine the ginger, spring onions, chives, lime rind and juice, sherry and soy sauce. Add the olive oil and whisk to mix. Season and set aside.

2 Preheat the grill. Sprinkle the tuna steaks with salt and pepper.

3 ▼ Arrange the tuna steaks on the rack in the grill pan. Grill about 3 in (8 cm) from the heat for about 5 minutes on each side, until the fish flakes easily when tested with a fork.

4 Arrange the cooked fish on a warmed serving platter or individual plates. Spoon the dressing over the fish and serve.

Fish with Orange and Caper Sauce (top), Tuna with Oriental Dressing

Crispy Cod Steaks with Tomato Sauce

SERVES 4

3 tbsp cornmeal, or polenta

½ tsp salt

¼ tsp hot chilli powder

4 cod steaks, each 1 in (2.5 cm) thick (about 1½ lb/700 g)

2 tbsp vegetable oil

fresh basil sprigs, for garnishing

FOR THE TOMATO SAUCE

2 tbsp olive oil

1 shallot, or ½ small onion, finely chopped

1 garlic clove, crushed

1 lb (450 g) ripe tomatoes, chopped, or 1 16 oz (450 g) can chopped tomatoes

⅛ tsp sugar

2 fl oz (65 ml) dry white wine

2 tbsp chopped fresh basil, or ½ tsp dried basil

salt and pepper

1 For the sauce, heat the oil in a saucepan. Add the shallot or onion and the garlic and cook until soft, about 5 minutes. Stir in the tomatoes, sugar, wine and basil. Bring to a boil. Simmer until thickened, 10–15 minutes.

2 ▲ Work the sauce through a vegetable mill or sieve until smooth. Return it to the pan. Season with salt and pepper. Set aside.

3 ▲ Combine the cornmeal or polenta, salt and chilli powder on a sheet of greaseproof paper.

4 ▲ Rinse the cod steaks, then dip them on both sides into the cornmeal mixture, patting gently until evenly coated.

5 ▲ Heat the oil in a large frying pan. Add the cod steaks and cook until golden brown and the flesh will flake easily when tested with a fork, about 5 minutes on each side. Cook in batches if necessary. Meanwhile, reheat the tomato sauce.

6 Garnish the cod steaks with basil sprigs and serve with the tomato sauce.

Spicy Fish Steaks

SERVES 4

1 tsp onion powder
1 tsp garlic salt
2 tsp paprika
1 tsp ground cumin
1 tsp mustard powder
1 tsp cayenne
2 tsp dried thyme
2 tsp dried oregano
½ tsp salt
1 tsp pepper
4 swordfish steaks, or other firm fleshed fish (about 1½ lb/700 g)
2 oz (55 g) butter or margarine, melted
dill sprigs, for garnishing

1 In a small bowl, combine all the spices, herbs and seasonings.

2 ▲ Brush both sides of the fish steaks with some of the melted butter or margarine.

3 ▲ Coat both sides of the fish steaks with the seasoning mixture, rubbing it in well.

4 Heat a large heavy frying pan until a drop of water sprinkled on the surface sizzles, about 5 minutes.

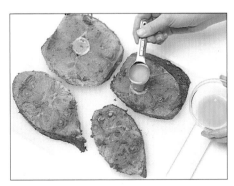

5 ▲ Drizzle 2 teaspoons of the remaining butter or margarine over the fish steaks. Add the steaks to the frying pan, butter-side down, and cook until the underside is blackened, 2–3 minutes.

6 ▲ Drizzle another 2 teaspoons of melted butter or margarine over the fish, then turn the steaks over. Cook until the second side is blackened and the fish flakes easily when tested with a fork, 2–3 minutes more.

7 Transfer the fish to warmed plates, garnish with dill and drizzle with the remaining butter or margarine.

Grilled Salmon with Lime Butter

SERVES 4

4 salmon steaks (about 1½ lb/700 g)

salt and pepper

FOR THE LIME BUTTER

2 oz (55 g) butter or margarine, at room temperature

1 tbsp chopped fresh coriander, or 1 tsp dried coriander

1 tsp finely grated lime rind

1 tbsp fresh lime juice

1 For the lime butter, combine the butter or margarine, coriander and lime rind and juice in a bowl. Mix well with a fork.

2 ▲ Transfer the lime butter to a piece of greaseproof paper and shape into a log. Roll in the paper until smooth and round. Refrigerate until firm, about 1 hour.

3 Preheat the grill.

4 ▼ Sprinkle the salmon steaks with salt and pepper. Arrange them on the rack in the grill pan. Grill about 3 in (8 cm) from the heat, 5 minutes on each side.

5 Unwrap the lime butter and cut into 4 pieces. Top each salmon steak with a pat of lime butter and serve.

Fish Fillets with Citrus Sauce

SERVES 6

½–1 oz (15–30 g) butter or margarine, melted

2 lb (900 g) sole fillets

salt and pepper

1 tsp grated lemon rind

1 tsp grated orange rind

2 tbsp fresh orange juice

3 fl oz (85 ml) whipping cream

1 tbsp chopped fresh basil

fresh basil sprigs, for garnishing

1 Preheat a 350°F/180°C/Gas 4 oven. Generously grease a large baking dish with the butter or margarine.

~ **VARIATION** ~

Use an equal amount of grapefruit rind and juice to replace the lemon and orange.

2 ▲ Lay the fish fillets skin-side down in the baking dish, in one layer. Sprinkle with salt and pepper.

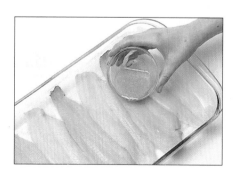

3 ▲ In a small bowl, combine the lemon and orange rinds and orange juice. Pour the mixture over the fish.

4 Bake until the fish flakes easily when tested with a fork, 15–20 minutes. Transfer the fish to a warmed serving platter.

5 ▲ Strain the juices from the baking dish into a small saucepan. Stir in the cream and chopped basil. Boil until thickened, about 5 minutes.

6 Spoon the citrus sauce over the fish fillets. Garnish with basil sprigs and serve.

Grilled Salmon with Lime Butter (top), Fish Fillets with Citrus Sauce

Sweet and Spicy Salmon Fillets

SERVES 6

2 lb (900 g) salmon fillet, cut in 6 pieces

4 fl oz (125 ml) honey

2 fl oz (65 ml) soy sauce

juice of 1 lime or lemon

1 tbsp sesame oil

¼ tsp crushed dried chilli pepper

¼ tsp crushed black peppercorns

~ COOK'S TIP ~

The acid in the citrus juice begins to 'cook' the fish, so grilling on one side only is sufficient.

1 Place the salmon pieces skin-side down in a large baking dish, in one layer.

2 ▲ In a bowl, combine the honey, soy sauce, lime or lemon juice, sesame oil, crushed chilli pepper and peppercorns.

3 ▲ Pour the mixture over the fish. Cover and let marinate 30 minutes.

4 Preheat the grill. Remove the fish from the marinade and arrange on the rack in the grill pan, skin-side down. Grill about 3 in (8 cm) from the heat until the fish flakes easily when tested with a fork, 6–8 minutes.

Cod Steaks with Pepper Crust

SERVES 4

1 tsp each pink, white and green peppercorns

1½ oz (45 g) butter or margarine

4 cod steaks, each 1 in (2.5 cm) thick (about 1 lb/450 g)

salt

4 fl oz (125 ml) fish stock

4 fl oz (125 ml) whipping cream

3 tbsp chopped fresh chives

1 ▼ Wrap the peppercorns in a tea towel or heavy plastic bag and crush with a rolling pin.

2 Melt the butter or margarine in a large frying pan. Remove from the heat. Brush the cod steaks with some of the butter or margarine.

3 ▲ Press the crushed peppercorns onto both sides of the cod steaks. Season with salt.

4 Heat the frying pan. Add the cod steaks and cook over medium-low heat until the fish flakes easily when tested with a fork, about 4 minutes on each side. Transfer the steaks to a warmed serving platter.

5 ▲ Add the stock and cream to the frying pan and bring to the boil, stirring well. Boil until reduced by half, about 5 minutes. Remove from the heat and stir in the chives.

6 Pour the sauce over the fish and serve immediately.

~ COOK'S TIP ~

If pink and green peppercorns are not available, use 1½ tsps each of white and black peppercorns.

Sweet and Spicy Salmon Fillets (top), Cod Steaks with Pepper Crust

Breaded Fish with Tartare Sauce

SERVES 4

2 oz (55 g) dry breadcrumbs

1 tsp dried oregano

½ tsp cayenne pepper

8 fl oz (250 ml) milk

2 tsp salt

4 pieces of cod fillet (about 1½ lb/ 700 g)

1½ oz (45 g) butter or margarine, melted

FOR THE TARTARE SAUCE

4 fl oz (125 ml) mayonnaise

½ tsp Dijon mustard

1–2 pickled gherkins, finely chopped

1 tbsp drained capers, chopped

1 tsp chopped fresh parsley

1 tsp chopped fresh chives

1 tsp chopped fresh tarragon

salt and pepper

1 Preheat a 450°F/230°C/Gas 8 oven. Grease a shallow ovenproof baking dish.

2 ▲ Combine the breadcrumbs, oregano and cayenne on a plate and blend together. Mix the milk with the salt in a bowl, stirring well to dissolve the salt.

3 ▲ Dip the pieces of cod fillet in the milk, then transfer to the plate and coat with the breadcrumb mixture.

4 ▲ Arrange the coated fish in the prepared baking dish, in one layer. Drizzle the melted butter or margarine over the fish.

5 Bake until the fish flakes easily when tested with a fork, about 10–15 minutes.

6 ▲ Meanwhile, for the tartare sauce, combine all the ingredients in a small bowl. Stir gently to mix well.

7 Serve the fish hot, accompanied by the tartare sauce.

Stuffed Sole

SERVES 4

8 skinless sole fillets (about 1 lb/450 g)

½ oz (15 g) butter or margarine, cut into 8 pieces

2 fl oz (65 ml) dry white wine

paprika, for garnishing

FOR THE STUFFING

1 oz (30 g) butter or margarine

1 small onion, finely chopped

1 handful of fresh spinach leaves, shredded

2 tbsp pine kernels, toasted

2 tbsp raisins

2 tbsp fresh breadcrumbs

⅛ tsp ground cinnamon

salt and pepper

1 Preheat a 400°F/200°C/Gas 6 oven. Butter a shallow baking dish.

2 ▲ For the stuffing, melt the butter or margarine in a small saucepan. Add the onion and cook over medium heat until softened, about 5 minutes. Stir in the spinach and cook, stirring constantly, until the spinach wilts and renders its liquid.

~ **VARIATION** ~

Use plaice instead of sole in this recipe, or try stuffing fillets of lean freshwater fish such as trout or perch.

3 Add the pine kernels, raisins, breadcrumbs, cinnamon and a little salt and pepper. Raise the heat and cook until most of the liquid has evaporated, stirring constantly. Remove from the heat.

4 ▲ Sprinkle the sole fillets with salt and pepper. Place a spoonful of the spinach stuffing at one end of each fillet. Roll up and secure with a wooden cocktail stick, if necessary.

5 ▲ Place the sole rolls in the prepared baking dish. Put a small piece of butter or margarine on each roll. Pour the wine over the fish. Cover the baking dish with foil and bake until the fish flakes easily when tested with a fork, about 15 minutes.

6 Serve on warmed plates with a little of the cooking juices spooned over the fish. Garnish with paprika, if wished.

Fish Fillets with Orange and Tomato Sauce

SERVES 4

3 tbsp plain flour

salt and pepper

4 fillets of firm white fish such as cod, sea bass, sole etc (about 1½ lb/700 g)

½ oz (15 g) butter or margarine

2 tbsp olive oil

1 onion, sliced

2 garlic cloves, chopped

¼ tsp ground cumin

1¼ lb (575 g) tomatoes, peeled, seeded and chopped, or 14 oz (400 g) canned chopped tomatoes

4 fl oz (125 ml) fresh orange juice

orange wedges, for garnishing

1 ▼ Put the flour on a plate and season with salt and pepper. Coat the fish fillets lightly with the seasoned flour, shaking off any excess.

2 Heat the butter or margarine and half the oil in a large frying pan. Add the fish fillets to the pan and cook until golden brown and the flesh flakes easily when tested with a fork, about 3 minutes on each side.

3 ▲ When the fish is cooked, transfer to a warmed serving platter. Cover with foil and keep warm while making the sauce.

4 ▲ Heat the remaining oil in the pan. Add the onion and garlic and cook until softened, about 5 minutes.

5 ▲ Stir in the cumin, tomatoes and orange juice. Bring to the boil and cook until thickened, about 10 minutes, stirring frequently.

6 Garnish the fish with orange wedges. Pass the sauce separately.

Baked Trout

SERVES 4

1 oz (30 g) butter or margarine
1 onion, chopped
1 celery stick, diced
2 slices of fresh bread, cut in ½ in (1 cm) cubes
1 tbsp fresh thyme, or 1 tsp dried thyme
salt and pepper
4 trout, cleaned (each about 8 oz/225 g)
8 rashers of bacon, rinded
celery leaves or parsley, for garnishing

1 Preheat a 450°F/230°C/Gas 8 oven.

2 ▲ Melt the butter or margarine in a frying pan. Add the onion and celery and cook until softened, about 5 minutes. Remove the pan from the heat. Add the bread cubes and thyme, and season with salt and pepper to taste. Stir to mix well.

3 ▲ Season the cavity of each trout with salt and pepper.

4 ▲ Stuff each trout with the bread mixture, dividing it evenly between the fish. If necessary, secure the openings with wooden cocktail sticks.

5 ▼ Wrap 2 bacon rashers around each stuffed trout. Arrange in a baking dish, in one layer.

6 Bake until the fish flakes easily when tested with a fork and the bacon is crisp, 35–40 minutes. Serve garnished with celery leaves or sprigs of parsley.

Halibut with Fruity Sauce

SERVES 4

4 halibut steaks (about 1½ lb/700 g)

1 oz (30 g) butter or margarine, melted

salt and pepper

fresh mint sprigs, for garnishing

FOR THE SAUCE

2½ oz (70 g) fresh pineapple, finely diced

2 tbsp diced red pepper

1 tbsp finely chopped red onion

finely grated rind of 1 lemon

1 tbsp lemon juice

1 tsp honey

2 tbsp chopped fresh mint

1 For the sauce, combine the pineapple, red pepper, red onion, lemon rind and juice and honey in a small bowl. Stir to mix. Cover with cling film and refrigerate for 30 minutes.

2 Preheat the grill.

3 ▲ Brush the halibut with butter or margarine and sprinkle with salt and pepper. Arrange on the rack in the grill pan, buttered-side up.

4 Grill the steaks about 3 in (8 cm) from the heat, turning once and brushing with the remaining butter or margarine, about 5 minutes on each side. Transfer to warmed serving plates.

5 ▲ Stir the chopped mint into the sauce. Garnish the halibut with mint sprigs and serve with the sauce.

Thick and Creamy Fish Stew

SERVES 4

3 thick-cut rashers of bacon, cut into small pieces

1 large onion, chopped

2 large potatoes, cut in ¾ in (2 cm) cubes (about 1½ lb/700 g)

salt and pepper

1¾ pt (1 litre) fish stock

1 lb (450 g) skinless haddock or cod fillet, cut into 1 in (2.5 cm) cubes

2 tbsp chopped fresh parsley

1 tbsp chopped fresh chives

8 fl oz (250 ml) whipping cream or milk

1 Fry the bacon in a deep saucepan until the fat is rendered. Add the onion and potatoes and cook over a low heat, without browning, about 10 minutes. Season to taste with salt and pepper.

2 ▲ Pour off excess fat from the pan. Add the fish stock to the pan and bring to the boil. Simmer until the vegetables are tender, 15–20 minutes.

3 ▲ Stir in the cubes of fish, the parsley and chives. Simmer until the fish is just cooked, 3–4 minutes.

4 Stir the cream or milk into the chowder and reheat gently. Season to taste and serve immediately.

Halibut with Fruity Sauce (top), Thick and Creamy Fish Stew

Crab Cakes

SERVES 3 OR 6

1 lb (450 g) fresh white crab meat

1 egg, well beaten

1 tsp Dijon mustard

2 tsp prepared horseradish

2 tsp Worcestershire sauce

8 spring onions, finely chopped

3 tbsp chopped fresh parsley

3 oz (85 g) fresh breadcrumbs

salt and pepper

1 tbsp whipping cream (optional)

2 oz (55 g) dry breadcrumbs

1½ oz (45 g) butter or margarine

lemon wedges, for serving

1 In a mixing bowl, combine the crab meat, egg, mustard, horseradish, Worcestershire sauce, spring onions, parsley, fresh breadcrumbs and seasoning. Mix gently, leaving the pieces of crab meat as large as possible. If the mixture is too dry to hold together, add the cream.

2 ▲ Divide the crab mixture into 6 portions and shape.

3 ▲ Put the dry breadcrumbs on a plate. Coat the crab cakes on both sides with the breadcrumbs.

4 Melt the butter or margarine in a frying pan. Fry the crab cakes until golden, about 3 minutes on each side. Add more fat if necessary.

5 Serve 1 or 2 per person, with lemon wedges.

Baked Stuffed Crab

SERVES 4

4 freshly cooked crabs

1 celery stick, diced

1 spring onion, finely chopped

1 small fresh green chilli pepper, seeded and finely chopped

3 fl oz (85 ml) mayonnaise

2 tbsp fresh lemon juice

1 tbsp chopped fresh chives

salt and pepper

1 oz (30 g) fresh breadcrumbs

2 oz (55 g) Cheddar cheese, grated

1 oz (30 g) butter or margarine, melted

parsley sprigs, for garnishing

1 Preheat a 375°F/190°C/Gas 5 oven.

2 ▼ Pull the claws and legs from each crab. Separate the body from the shell. Scoop out the meat from the shell. Discard the feathery gills and the intestines; remove the meat and coral from the body. Crack the claws and remove the meat.

3 Scrub the shells. Cut into the seam on the underside with scissors. The inner part of the shell should break off cleanly along the seam, enlarging the opening. Rinse the shells and dry them well.

4 In a bowl, combine the crab meat, celery, spring onion, chilli pepper, mayonnaise, lemon juice and chives. Season with salt and pepper to taste and mix well.

5 In another bowl, toss together the breadcrumbs, cheese, and melted butter or margarine.

6 ▲ Pile the crab mixture into the shells. Sprinkle with the cheese mixture. Bake until golden brown, about 20 minutes. Serve hot, garnished with parsley sprigs.

Crab Cakes (top), Baked Stuffed Crab

Paella

Serves 6

4 tbsp olive oil
10 oz (300 g) short-grain rice
1 large onion, chopped
1 red pepper, seeded and chopped
12 oz (350 g) squid, cleaned and cut into rings (optional)
18 fl oz (500 ml) fish or chicken stock
4 fl oz (125 ml) dry white wine
½ tsp saffron strands
1 large garlic clove, crushed
8 fl oz (250 ml) canned chopped tomatoes
1 bay leaf
¼ tsp finely grated lemon rind
4 oz (115 g) chorizo or other spicy cooked sausage, cut into ¼ in (5 mm) slices
salt and pepper
7 oz (200 g) fresh or frozen green peas
12 oz (350 g) monkfish, skinned and cut into 1 in (2.5 cm) pieces
24 mussels, well scrubbed
12 raw or cooked prawns, peeled and deveined

1 ▼ Heat the oil in a large frying pan or paella pan. Add the rice and cook over a medium-high heat until it begins to colour, stirring frequently.

2 ▲ Stir in the onion and pepper and cook 2–3 minutes longer.

3 ▲ Add the squid, if using, and cook, stirring occasionally, until it is lightly browned.

4 Stir in the stock, wine, saffron, and garlic. Bring to the boil.

5 ▲ Add the tomatoes, bay leaf, lemon rind, and sausage. Season with salt and pepper. Return to the boil, then reduce the heat. Cover and simmer until the rice has absorbed most of the liquid, about 15 minutes.

6 ▲ Add the peas, monkfish and mussels to the rice. Push the mussels down into the rice.

7 ▲ Gently stir in the prawns. Cover and continue cooking until the mussels have opened and the rice is tender, about 5 minutes. Raw prawns should have turned bright pink.

8 Taste and adjust the seasoning. Serve immediately in a heated serving dish or from the paella pan, if using.

~ COOK'S TIP ~

This recipe can be doubled to feed a crowd. Be sure to use a larger pan, such as a wide shallow flameproof casserole. The final simmering, after the pan has been covered (step 5), can be done in a preheated 375°F/190°C/Gas 5 oven. If using a paella pan, cover with foil.

Seafood and Vegetable Stir-Fry

SERVES 4

1 lb (450 g) rice vermicelli

2 tbsp oil drained from sun-dried tomatoes

4 fl oz (125 ml) sun-dried tomatoes preserved in oil, drained and sliced

4 spring onions, cut diagonally in ½ in (1 cm) lengths

2 large carrots, cut in thin sticks

1 courgette, cut in thin sticks

8 oz (225 g) raw prawns, peeled and deveined, or cooked peeled prawns

8 oz (225 g) scallops, shelled

1 in (2.5 cm) piece of fresh root ginger, peeled and finely grated

3 tbsp fresh lemon juice

3 tbsp chopped fresh basil, or 1 tsp dried basil

salt and pepper

1 ▲ Bring a large saucepan of water to the boil. Add the rice vermicelli and cook until tender (check packet instructions for timing). Drain, rinse with boiling water, and drain again thoroughly. Keep warm.

2 ▲ Heat the oil in a wok over high heat. Add the tomatoes, spring onions and carrots and stir-fry 5 minutes.

3 ▲ Add the courgette, raw prawns, scallops and grated ginger. Stir-fry 3 minutes.

4 ▲ Add the lemon juice, basil and salt and pepper to taste and stir well. Add the cooked prawns, if using. Stir-fry until the prawns are all pink and hot, about 2 more minutes.

5 Serve on the rice vermicelli.

Chunky Seafood Stew

SERVES 6

3 tbsp olive oil

2 large onions, chopped

1 small green pepper, seeded and sliced

3 carrots, chopped

3 garlic cloves, crushed

2 tbsp tomato purée

2 × 14 oz (400 g) cans chopped tomatoes

3 tbsp chopped fresh parsley

1 tsp fresh thyme, or ¼ tsp dried thyme

1 tbsp chopped fresh basil, or 1 tsp dried basil

4 fl oz (125 ml) dry white wine

1 lb (450 g) raw prawns, peeled and deveined, or cooked peeled prawns

3 lb (1.35 kg) mussels or clams (in shells), or a mixture of both, thoroughly cleaned

2 lb (900 g) halibut or other firm, white fish fillets, cut in 2–3 in (5–8 cm) pieces

12 fl oz (375 ml) fish stock or water

salt and pepper

extra chopped fresh herbs, for garnishing

1 ▲ Heat the oil in a flameproof casserole. Add the onions, green pepper, carrots and garlic and cook until tender, about 5 minutes.

2 Add the tomato purée, canned tomatoes, herbs and wine and stir well to combine. Bring to the boil and simmer 20 minutes.

3 ▲ Add the raw prawns, mussels, clams, fish pieces and stock or water. Season with salt and pepper.

4 ▲ Bring back to the boil, then simmer until the prawns turn pink, the fish flakes easily and the mussels and clams open, 5–6 minutes. Add cooked prawns for last 2 minutes.

5 Serve in large soup plates, garnished with chopped herbs.

Spicy Tomato Prawns

SERVES 4

2 oz (55 g) butter or margarine

3 garlic cloves, crushed

1 large onion, finely chopped

1 green pepper, seeded and diced

2 sticks celery, chopped

16 fl oz (450 ml) canned chopped
tomatoes

1 tsp sugar

2 tsp salt

1 bay leaf

1½ tsp fresh thyme leaves, or ½ tsp
dried thyme

¼ tsp cayenne pepper

2 lb (900 g) raw prawns, peeled and
deveined, or cooked peeled prawns

½ tsp grated lemon rind

2 tbsp fresh lemon juice

pepper

1 Heat the butter or margarine in a
flameproof casserole. Add the garlic,
onion, pepper and celery and cook
until softened, about 5 minutes.

2 ▲ Add the tomatoes, sugar, salt,
bay leaf, thyme and cayenne. Bring to
the boil. Reduce the heat and simmer
10 minutes.

3 ▲ Stir in the prawns, lemon rind
and juice and pepper to taste. Cover
and simmer until raw prawns turn
pink, about 5 minutes, or until cooked
prawns are hot, about 2 minutes.

4 Serve immediately on a bed of
freshly cooked rice.

Prawns in Creamy Mustard Sauce

SERVES 4

2 oz (55 g) butter or margarine

2 lb (900 g) raw prawns, peeled and
deveined, or cooked peeled prawns

1 small onion, finely chopped

4 spring onions, cut diagonally in ⅛ in
(3 mm) lengths

2 tbsp fresh lemon juice

4 fl oz (125 ml) dry white wine

4 fl oz (125 ml) whipping cream

2 tbsp whole-grain mustard

salt and pepper

1 Melt half the butter or margarine in
a frying pan over high heat. Add raw
prawns, if using, and cook until they
turn pink and opaque, about 2
minutes, stirring constantly. Remove
with a slotted spoon and set aside.

2 Melt the remaining butter or
margarine in the frying pan. Add the
onion and spring onions and cook
until softened, 3–4 minutes, stirring
frequently.

3 ▲ Stir in the lemon juice and
wine. Bring to the boil, scraping the
bottom of the pan with a wooden
spoon to mix in the cooking juices.

4 ▲ Add the cream. Simmer until
the mixture thickens, 3–4 minutes,
stirring frequently. Stir in the
mustard.

5 Return the fried prawns to the pan
and reheat briefly. Add cooked
prawns at this stage and heat through,
about 2 minutes. Season with salt and
pepper and serve.

Spicy Tomato Prawns (top), Prawns in Creamy Mustard Sauce

Special Occasion Seafood Platter

SERVES 6

salt

6 × 1 lb (450 g) lobsters, fresh, frozen and thawed, or cooked

2 lb (900 g) button onions, peeled

2 lb (900 g) small red potatoes

3 dozen small hard-shelled clams, or mussels, thoroughly cleaned

6 sweetcorn cobs, trimmed

8 oz (225 g) butter or margarine

3 tbsp chopped fresh chives

1 Put 1 in (2.5 cm) of salted water in the bottom of a deep pan. Put the fresh lobsters on top. Cooked lobsters should be steamed with 1 in (2.5 cm) of salted water in a separate pan 5 minutes only to heat through.

2 Add the onions and potatoes. Cover the pan tightly and bring the water to the boil.

3 ▲ After 10 minutes, add the clams or mussels and the sweetcorn cobs. Cover again and cook until the lobster shells are red and the potatoes are tender, 15–20 minutes longer.

4 ▲ Meanwhile, in a small saucepan melt the butter or margarine and stir in the chives.

5 Serve the lobsters and clams or mussels with the vegetables, accompanied by the chive butter.

Seafood Kebabs

SERVES 4

16 scallops, shelled, or frozen and thawed

½ tsp ground ginger

1 × 8 oz (225 g) can pineapple chunks in juice, drained and juice reserved

1 small fresh red chilli pepper, seeded and chopped

grated rind and juice of 1 lime or lemon

16 mange-tout

16 cherry tomatoes

8 baby courgettes, halved

1 Put the scallops in a bowl. Add the ginger, the juice from the pineapple, the chilli pepper and lime or lemon rind and juice and stir well. Cover and let marinate at room temperature about 20 minutes, or 2 hours in the refrigerator.

2 Preheat the grill.

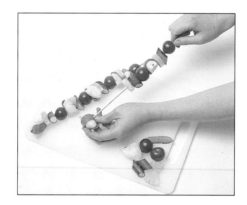

3 ▲ Drain the scallops, reserving their marinade. Wrap a mange-tout around a scallop and thread onto 1 of 4 skewers. Thread on a cherry tomato, a piece of courgette, and a piece of pineapple, followed by another mange-tout-wrapped scallop. Repeat until all the ingredients have been used.

4 ▲ Lay the kebabs in the grill pan and brush with the reserved marinade.

5 Grill about 3 in (8 cm) from the heat, brushing frequently with the marinade and turning occasionally, until the scallops are opaque, 4–5 minutes.

6 Serve immediately, on a bed of cooked rice, if wished.

Special Occasion Seafood Platter (top), Seafood Kebabs

MEAT & POULTRY

~

The wide range of different meats – beef, lamb and pork, as well as chicken and turkey – lends itself to endless variations. Ring the changes with these delicious recipes, from traditional grills and roasts to exotically spicy dishes.

Layered Meat and Fruit Loaf

SERVES 6

1½ lb (700 g) minced beef

8 oz (225 g) minced pork

2 eggs, lightly beaten

2 oz (55 g) fresh breadcrumbs

¼ tsp ground cinnamon

salt and pepper

FOR THE STUFFING

½ oz (15 g) butter or margarine

1 small onion, chopped

1½ oz (45 g) chopped dried figs

1½ oz (45 g) chopped dried apricots

1½ oz (45 g) sultanas

1 oz (30 g) pine kernels

4 fl oz (125 ml) dry white wine

2 tbsp chopped fresh parsley

1 Preheat a 350°F/180°C/Gas 4 oven.

2 ▼ For the stuffing, melt the butter or margarine in a small frying pan. Add the onion and cook until softened, about 5 minutes. Stir in the figs, apricots, raisins, pine kernels and wine. Bring to the boil and boil to evaporate the liquid, about 5 minutes. Remove from the heat and stir in the parsley. Set aside.

3 In a bowl, mix together the beef, pork, eggs, breadcrumbs, cinnamon and a little salt and pepper.

4 ▲ Press half of the meat mixture in a 9 × 5 in (23 × 13 cm) loaf tin. Spoon the stuffing over the meat. Spread the remaining meat mixture on top and press down gently.

5 Cover the tin with foil. Bake 1¼ hours. Pour off any excess fat from the tin. Let the meat loaf cool slightly before serving.

Steak with Spicy Mushroom Sauce

SERVES 4

2½ oz (70 g) butter or margarine

1 lb (450 g) mushrooms, quartered

1 shallot or ½ small onion, finely chopped

3 tbsp chopped fresh parsley

salt and pepper

4 sirloin steaks, each about 1 in (2.5 cm) thick

1 onion, thinly sliced

⅛ tsp crushed dried chilli pepper

⅛ tsp cayenne pepper

dash of chilli sauce

2 tsp Worcestershire sauce

2 tsp sugar

5 fl oz (150 ml) brandy

8 fl oz (250 ml) beef stock

1 ▼ Melt 1 oz (30 g) of the butter or margarine in a frying pan. Add the mushrooms and shallot and cook until softened, about 5 minutes. Drain off the excess liquid. Sprinkle the mushrooms with the parsley and a little salt and pepper. Set aside.

2 Preheat the grill. Sprinkle the steaks with salt and pepper and arrange them on the rack in the grill pan. Set aside.

3 Melt the remaining butter or margarine in a saucepan. Add the onion and cook until softened, about 5 minutes. Stir in the dried chilli pepper, cayenne, chilli sauce, Worcestershire sauce, sugar and brandy. Bring to the boil and boil until the sauce is reduced by half.

4 Meanwhile, grill the steaks about 3 in (8 cm) from the heat, 5 minutes on each side for medium-rare, 8 minutes on each side for medium.

5 While the steaks are cooking, add the stock to the sauce and boil again to reduce by half. Season to taste with salt and pepper. Stir in the cooked mushrooms.

6 Transfer the steaks to heated plates and spoon the sauce on top.

Layered Meat and Fruit Loaf (top), Steak with Spicy Mushroom Sauce

Cheeseburgers with Spicy Avocado Relish

SERVES 6

2 lb (900 g) minced beef

salt and pepper

6 slices of Gruyère or Cheddar cheese

6 hamburger buns with sesame seeds, split and toasted

2 large tomatoes, sliced

FOR THE AVOCADO RELISH

1 large ripe avocado

1 spring onion, chopped

2 tsp fresh lemon juice

1 tsp chilli powder

2 tbsp chopped fresh tomato

1 To make the relish, peel the avocado, discard the stone, and mash the flesh with a fork. Stir in the spring onion, lemon juice, chilli powder, and chopped tomato. Set aside.

2 Preheat the grill.

3 ▼ Handling the beef as little as possible, divide it into 6 equal portions. Shape each portion into a burger ¾ in (2 cm) thick and season.

4 Arrange the burgers on the rack in the grill pan. Grill about 3 in (8 cm) from the heat, 5 minutes on each side for medium-rare, 8 minutes on each side for well-done.

5 ▲ Top each hamburger with a slice of cheese and grill until melted, about 30 seconds.

6 Place a hamburger in each toasted bun. Top with a slice of tomato and a spoonful of avocado relish and serve.

Chilli con Carne

SERVES 8

3 tbsp vegetable oil

1 large onion, chopped

2 lb (900 g) minced beef

4 garlic cloves, crushed

1 tbsp light brown sugar

2–3 tbsp chilli powder

1 tsp ground cumin

1 tsp each salt and pepper

1 × 5 oz (140 g) can tomato purée

8 fl oz (250 ml) beer

15 fl oz (450 ml) fresh tomatoes, blanched, skinned, cooked and sieved

12 oz (350 g) cooked or canned red kidney beans, rinsed and drained

FOR SERVING

1 lb (450 g) spaghetti, broken in half

8 fl oz (250 ml) soured cream

8 oz (225 g) Cheddar or Gruyère cheese, grated

1 Heat the oil in a deep saucepan and cook the onion until softened, about 5 minutes. Add the beef and cook until browned, breaking up the meat with the side of a spoon.

2 ▼ Stir in the garlic, brown sugar, chilli powder, cumin, salt and pepper. Add the tomato purée, beer and sieved tomatoes and stir to mix. Bring to the boil. Reduce the heat, cover, and simmer 50 minutes.

3 ▲ Stir in the kidney beans and simmer 5 minutes longer, uncovered.

4 Meanwhile, cook the spaghetti in a large pot of boiling salted water until just tender (check packet instructions for cooking time). Drain.

5 To serve, put the spaghetti into a warmed bowl. Ladle the chilli over the spaghetti and top with some of the soured cream and grated cheese. Serve the remaining soured cream and cheese separately.

Cheeseburgers with Spicy Avocado Relish (top), Chilli con Carne

Old-Fashioned Beef Stew

SERVES 6

3 tbsp vegetable oil

1 large onion, sliced

2 carrots, chopped

1 celery stick, chopped

1 oz (30 g) plain flour

3 tbsp paprika

2 lb (900 g) braising steak, cubed

2 tbsp tomato purée

8 fl oz (250 ml) red wine

15 fl oz (450 ml) beef stock

1 sprig of fresh thyme, or 1 tsp dried thyme

1 bay leaf

salt and pepper

3 medium potatoes, cut into 1½ in (3 cm) pieces

3 oz (85 g) button mushrooms, quartered

1 Preheat a 375°F/190°C/Gas 5 oven.

2 ▼ Heat half the oil in a large flameproof casserole. Add the onion, carrots and celery and cook until softened, about 5 minutes. Remove the vegetables with a slotted spoon and set aside.

3 ▲ Combine the flour and paprika in a plastic bag. Add the beef cubes and shake to coat them with the seasoned flour.

4 Heat the remaining oil in the casserole. Add the beef cubes and brown well on all sides, about 10 minutes.

5 Return the vegetables to the casserole. Stir in the tomato purée, red wine, stock, herbs and seasoning. Bring to the boil.

6 ▲ Stir in the potatoes. Cover the casserole and transfer it to the oven. Cook 1 hour.

7 Stir in the mushrooms and continue cooking until the beef is very tender, about 30 minutes longer. Discard the bay leaf before serving.

Beef and Vegetable Stir-Fry

SERVES 4

| 2–3 tsp chilli powder |
| 1 tsp ground cumin |
| ½ tsp dried oregano |
| salt and pepper |
| 1 lb (450 g) topside of beef, cut into thin strips |
| 2 tbsp vegetable oil |
| 5 spring onions, cut diagonally into 1 in (2.5 cm) lengths |
| 1 small green pepper, seeded and thinly sliced |
| 1 small red pepper, seeded and thinly sliced |
| 1 small yellow pepper, seeded and thinly sliced |
| 4 oz (115 g) baby corn cobs, halved lengthwise, or 8 oz (225 g) canned sweetcorn, drained |
| 4 garlic cloves, crushed |
| 2 tbsp fresh lime or lemon juice |
| 2 tbsp chopped fresh coriander |

1 ▼ In a medium bowl, combine the spices, oregano and a little salt and pepper. Rub the mixture into the beef strips.

2 Heat half the oil in a wok or large frying pan over high heat. Add the beef strips and stir-fry until well browned on all sides, 3–4 minutes. Remove the beef from the wok with a slotted spoon and keep hot.

3 ▲ Heat the remaining oil in the wok and add the spring onions, peppers, sweetcorn and garlic. Stir-fry until the vegetables are just tender, about 3 minutes.

4 ▼ Return the beef to the wok and toss briefly to mix with the vegetables and heat it through. Stir in the lime or lemon juice and coriander and serve.

Boiled Beef Platter

SERVES 6

2–2½ lb (about 1 kg) salted brisket

1 tsp black peppercorns

2 bay leaves

1 small swede, about 1 lb (450 g), cut into pieces

8 button onions

8 small red potatoes

3 carrots, cut into sticks

1 small head of green cabbage, cut into 6 wedges

FOR THE SAUCE

3 fl oz (85 ml) red wine vinegar

2 oz (55 g) sugar

1 tbsp mustard powder

about 2 oz (55 g) butter or margarine

salt and pepper

1 Put the brisket in a large pan. Add the peppercorns and bay leaves and cover with water. Bring to the boil. Reduce the heat and simmer until the beef is almost tender, about 2 hours.

2 ▼ Add the swede, onions, potatoes and carrots. Bring the liquid back to the boil, then reduce the heat and cover the pan. Simmer 10 minutes.

3 Add the cabbage wedges. Cover and cook 15 minutes longer.

4 With a slotted spoon, remove the meat and vegetables from the pan and keep them hot. Reserve 12 fl oz (350 ml) of the cooking liquid.

5 ▲ For the sauce, combine the reserved cooking liquid, vinegar, sugar and mustard in a small saucepan. Bring to the boil, then reduce the heat and simmer until thickened, about 5 minutes. Remove the pan from the heat and swirl in the butter or margarine. Season to taste with salt and pepper.

6 Slice the beef and arrange with the vegetables on a warmed platter. Serve with the sauce in a sauceboat.

Steak Sandwiches with Onions

SERVES 3

3 pieces thinly cut rump steak (about 1 lb/450 g)

salt and pepper

1 oz (30 g) butter or margarine

2 tbsp vegetable oil

1 large onion, thinly sliced into rings

1 long French stick, split in half lengthwise, and cut into 3 sections

Dijon mustard, for serving

1 Sprinkle the steaks generously with salt and pepper.

2 ▲ Heat the butter or margarine and half the oil in a frying pan. Add the onion and cook until browned and crispy, about 8 minutes. Remove the onion with a slotted spoon and drain on kitchen paper. Add the remaining oil to the pan.

3 ▼ Add the steaks to the frying pan and cook until well browned, about 3 minutes, turning once.

4 Divide the steak and onions among the bottom halves of the bread sections, and put on the tops. Serve on warmed plates with mustard.

Boiled Beef Platter (top), Steak Sandwiches with Onions

Pork with Mustard and Pepper Sauce

SERVES 4

2 pork fillets, each about 12 oz (350 g)

1 oz (30 g) butter or margarine

1 tbsp olive oil

1 tbsp red wine vinegar

1 tbsp whole-grain mustard

3 tbsp whipping cream

1 tbsp green peppercorns in brine, drained

pinch salt

1 Cut the pork fillets across into 1 in (2.5 cm) thick slices.

2 ▼ Heat the butter or margarine and oil in a frying pan. Add the slices of pork and fry until browned and cooked through, 5–8 minutes on each side. Transfer the pork to a warmed serving plate and keep hot.

3 ▼ Add the vinegar and mustard to the pan and cook 1 minute, stirring with a wooden spoon to loosen any particles attached to the bottom.

4 Stir in the cream, peppercorns and salt. Boil 1 minute. Pour the sauce over the pork and serve immediately.

Pork Chops with Apple and Potato

SERVES 6

15 fl oz (450 ml) apple juice

8 oz (225 g) baking potatoes, peeled and cut into ½ in (1 cm) slices

8 oz (225 g) sweet potatoes, or swede, peeled and cut into ½ in (1 cm) slices

1 lb (450 g) apples, peeled, cored, and cut into ½ in (1 cm) slices

salt and pepper

1½ oz (45 g) plain flour

6 pork chops, cut 1 in (2.5 cm) thick, trimmed of excess fat

2 oz (55 g) butter or margarine

3 tbsp vegetable oil

6 fresh sage leaves

1 Preheat a 350°F/180°C/Gas 4 oven. Grease a 13 × 9 in (33 × 23 cm) baking dish.

2 In a small saucepan, bring the apple juice to the boil.

3 ▼ Arrange a row of baking-potato slices at a short end of the prepared dish. Arrange a row of sweet-potato slices next to the first row, slightly overlapping it, and then a row of apple slices. Repeat the alternating overlapping rows to fill the dish. Sprinkle with salt and pepper.

4 Pour the apple juice over the potato and apple slices. Cover the dish with foil and bake 40 minutes.

5 ▲ Meanwhile, season the flour with salt and pepper. Coat the chops with the seasoned flour, shaking off any excess. Melt the butter or margarine with the oil in a frying pan. Fry the chops until well browned, about 5 minutes on each side.

6 Uncover the baking dish. Arrange the chops on top of the potatoes and apples. Put a sage leaf on each chop.

7 Return to the oven, uncovered, and cook until the potatoes and pork chops are tender and most of the liquid is absorbed, about 1 hour.

Pork with Mustard and Pepper Sauce (top), Pork Chops with Apple and Potato

Pork Chops with Sauerkraut

SERVES 6

6 rashers of bacon, coarsely chopped
3 tbsp plain flour
salt and pepper
6 boned loin pork chops
2 tsp light brown sugar
1 garlic clove, crushed
1½ lb (700 g) sauerkraut, rinsed
1 tsp juniper berries
1 tsp black peppercorns
8 fl oz (250 ml) beer
8 fl oz (250 ml) chicken stock

1 Preheat a 350°F/180°C/Gas 4 oven.

2 ▼ In a frying pan, fry the bacon until just beginning to brown. With a slotted spoon, transfer the bacon to a casserole dish.

3 ▲ Season the flour with salt and pepper. Coat the pork chops with the seasoned flour, shaking off any excess. Brown the chops in the bacon fat, about 5 minutes on each side. Remove and drain on kitchen paper.

4 ▲ Add the brown sugar and garlic to the fat in the frying pan and cook, stirring, for 3 minutes. Add the sauerkraut, juniper berries and peppercorns.

5 ▲ Transfer the sauerkraut mixture to the casserole and mix with the bacon. Lay the pork chops on top. Pour the beer and chicken stock over the chops.

6 Place the casserole in the oven and cook until the chops are very tender, 45–55 minutes.

Barbecued Spareribs

SERVES 4

3 lb (1.35 kg) meaty pork spareribs

4 fl oz (125 ml) vegetable oil

½ tsp paprika

FOR THE SAUCE

3 oz (85 g) light brown sugar

2 tsp mustard powder

1 tsp salt

⅛ tsp pepper

½ tsp ground ginger

4 fl oz (125 ml) fresh tomatoes, skinned, cooked and sieved

4 fl oz (125 ml) orange juice

1 small onion, finely chopped

1 garlic clove, crushed

2 tbsp chopped fresh parsley

1 tbsp Worcestershire sauce

1 ▲ Preheat a 375°F/190°C/Gas 5 oven. Arrange the ribs in one layer in a roasting tin.

2 ▲ In a small bowl, combine the oil and paprika. Brush the mixture over the spareribs. Bake until the ribs are slightly crisp, 55–60 minutes.

3 ▼ Combine the sauce ingredients in a saucepan and bring to the boil. Simmer 5 minutes, stirring occasionally.

4 ▲ Pour off the fat from the roasting tin. Brush the ribs with half of the sauce and bake 20 minutes. Turn the ribs over and brush with the remaining sauce. Bake 20 minutes longer. Cut into sections for serving.

Spicy Pork on Tortilla Pancakes

SERVES 4

1 garlic clove, crushed
2 tbsp vegetable oil
3 fl oz (85 ml) fresh lime juice
3 tbsp Worcestershire sauce
⅛ tsp pepper
1¼ lb (575 g) pork cutlets, cut lengthwise into ⅜ in (1 cm) strips
1 large ripe avocado
4 tbsp finely chopped fresh coriander leaves
8 corn tortillas
1 onion, sliced
1 green pepper, seeded and sliced
black olives, for garnishing
FOR THE SALSA
8 oz (225 g) drained canned sweetcorn, or frozen sweetcorn, thawed
1 small red pepper, seeded and finely chopped
1 small red onion, thinly sliced
1 tsp honey
juice of 1 lime or lemon

1 ▼ In a medium bowl, combine the garlic, 1 tablespoon of the oil, the lime juice, Worcestershire sauce and pepper. Add the pork strips and toss to coat. Let marinate 10–20 minutes, stirring the strips at least once.

2 ▲ Meanwhile, combine all the ingredients for the salsa in a bowl and mix well. Set aside.

3 ▲ Cut the avocado in half and remove the stone. Scrape the flesh into a bowl and mash it with a fork. Stir in the chopped coriander.

4 ▲ Preheat the oven to 350°F/ 180°C/Gas 4. Wrap the corn tortillas in foil and heat them in the oven for 10 minutes.

5 ▲ Meanwhile, heat the remaining oil in a frying pan. Add the onion and green pepper slices and cook until softened, about 5 minutes.

6 ▲ Add the pork strips to the frying pan and fry briskly, turning occasionally, until cooked and browned, about 5 minutes.

7 ▲ To serve, place a spoonful of the avocado on each of the heated tortillas. Top with some of the pork mixture and a spoonful of the salsa. Garnish with an olive, and serve with more salsa, if wished.

Baked Sausages and Beans with Crispy Topping

SERVES 6

12 oz (350 g) dried haricot or white beans, soaked overnight and drained

1 onion, stuck with 4 cloves

1½ oz (45 g) butter or margarine

1 lb (450 g) pork link sausages

1 lb (450 g) garlic sausage, cut into ½ in (1 cm) slices

4 oz (115 g) bacon, chopped

1 large onion, finely chopped

2 garlic cloves, crushed

1 × 16 oz (450 g) can chopped tomatoes

5 oz (140 g) can tomato purée

2 fl oz (65 ml) maple syrup

2 tbsp dark brown sugar

½ tsp mustard powder

¼ tsp salt

pepper

1 oz (30 g) fresh breadcrumbs

1 ▲ Put the beans in a saucepan and cover with fresh cold water. Add the clove-studded onion. Bring to the boil and boil until the beans are just tender, about 1 hour. Drain the beans. Discard the onion.

2 Preheat a 350°F/180°C/Gas 4 oven.

3 ▲ Melt half of the butter or margarine in a large flameproof casserole. Add the sausages, bacon, onion and garlic and fry until the bacon and sausages are well browned.

4 ▲ Stir in the beans, tomatoes, tomato purée, maple syrup, brown sugar, mustard, salt and pepper to taste. Bring to the boil.

5 ▲ Sprinkle the breadcrumbs over the surface and dot with the remaining butter or margarine.

6 Transfer the casserole to the oven and bake until most of liquid has been absorbed by the beans and the top is crisp, about 1 hour.

Jambalaya

SERVES 6

2 tbsp vegetable oil
4 skinless boneless chicken breast halves, cut into chunks
1 lb (450 g) spicy cooked sausage, sliced
6 oz (170 g) smoked ham, cubed
1 large onion, chopped
2 celery sticks, chopped
2 green peppers, seeded and chopped
3 garlic cloves, crushed
8 fl oz (250 ml) canned chopped tomatoes
16 fl oz (450 ml) chicken stock
1 tsp cayenne pepper
1 sprig of fresh thyme, or ¼ tsp dried thyme
2 sprigs of flat-leaved parsley
1 bay leaf
10 oz (300 g) rice
salt and pepper
4 spring onions, finely chopped

1 ▼ Heat the oil in a large frying pan. Add the chicken chunks and sausage slices and cook until well browned, about 5 minutes. Stir in the ham cubes and cook 5 minutes longer.

2 Add the onion, celery, peppers, garlic, tomatoes, stock, cayenne, thyme, parsley and bay leaf to the frying pan. Bring to the boil, stirring well.

3 ▲ Stir in the rice, and add salt and and pepper to taste. When the liquid returns to the boil, reduce the heat and cover the pan tightly. Simmer 10 minutes.

4 Remove the pan from the heat and, without removing the lid, set aside for 20 minutes, to let the rice finish cooking.

5 ▲ Discard the bay leaf. Scatter the chopped spring onions on top of the jambalaya just before serving.

Ham and Asparagus with Cheese Sauce

SERVES 4

24 asparagus spears

1½ oz (45 g) butter or margarine

3 tbsp plain flour

12 fl oz (350 ml) milk

4 oz (115 g) Gruyère or Cheddar cheese, grated

⅛ tsp grated nutmeg

salt and pepper

12 thin slices of cooked ham or Parma ham

1 Trim any tough stalk ends from the asparagus. Bring a wide shallow pan of salted water to the boil. Add the asparagus and simmer until barely tender, 5–7 minutes. Drain the asparagus in a colander, rinse with cold water and spread out on kitchen paper to dry.

2 Preheat the grill. Grease a 13 × 9 in (33 × 23 cm) baking dish.

3 Melt the butter or margarine in a saucepan. Add the flour and cook 2 minutes, stirring. Stir in the milk. Bring to the boil, stirring constantly, and simmer until thickened, about 5 minutes.

4 ▲ Add three-quarters of the cheese to the sauce. Season to taste with nutmeg, salt and pepper. Keep warm.

5 ▲ Wrap a pair of asparagus spears in each slice of ham. Arrange in the prepared baking dish, in one layer.

6 Pour the sauce over the ham and asparagus rolls and sprinkle the remaining cheese on top. Grill about 3 in (8 cm) from the heat until bubbling and golden brown, about 5 minutes. Serve hot.

Gammon Steaks with Raisin Sauce

SERVES 4

2 oz (55 g) raisins

8 fl oz (250 ml) warm water

½ tsp instant coffee

1 tsp cornflour

1½ oz (45 g) butter or margarine

4 gammon steaks, about 4 oz (115 g) each, trimmed of excess fat

2 tsp dark brown sugar

2 tsp cider vinegar

2 tsp soy sauce

~ **VARIATION** ~

For a richer sauce, substitute an equal quantity of chopped prunes for the raisins.

1 ▼ In a small bowl, soak the raisins in half of the water to plump them, about 10 minutes.

2 Stir the coffee and cornflour into the remaining water until smooth.

3 Melt the butter or margarine in a large frying pan. Add the gammon steaks and cook over a medium-low heat until lightly browned, about 5 minutes on each side.

4 ▲ Transfer the cooked steaks to a heated serving dish.

5 Drain the raisins and add them to the frying pan. Stir the coffee mixture to recombine it, then add to the pan with the sugar, vinegar and soy sauce. Bring to the boil and simmer until slightly thickened, about 3 minutes, stirring constantly.

6 Spoon the raisin sauce over the gammon steaks and serve.

Ham and Asparagus with Cheese Sauce (top), Gammon Steaks with Raisin Sauce

Lamb Chops with Basil Sauce

SERVES 4

small bunch of fresh basil leaves

1 oz (30 g) pine kernels

2 garlic cloves

1 oz (30 g) Parmesan cheese, diced

4 fl oz (125 ml) extra-virgin olive oil

salt and pepper

4 lamb sirloin or chump chops, about 8 oz (225 g) each

fresh basil sprigs, for garnishing

1 In a food processor or blender, combine the basil, pine kernels, garlic and Parmesan cheese. Process until the ingredients are finely chopped. Gradually pour in the olive oil in a thin stream. Season to taste with salt and pepper. The sauce should be thin and creamy. Alternatively, use a mortar and pestle to make the sauce.

2 ▼ Put the lamb chops in a shallow dish that will hold them comfortably side by side. Pour the basil sauce over the chops. Turn to coat on both sides. Let marinate 1 hour.

3 Preheat the grill. Brush the rack in the grill pan with olive oil.

4 ▲ Transfer the chops to the grill rack. Grill about 3 in (8 cm) from the heat until well browned and cooked to taste, about 15 minutes, turning once. Serve garnished with fresh basil sprigs.

Lamb and Bean Stew

SERVES 6

9 oz (250 g) dried red kidney beans, soaked overnight and drained

2 tbsp vegetable oil

2 lb (900 g) lean boned lamb, cut into 1½ in (3 cm) cubes

1 large onion, chopped

1 bay leaf

1¼ pt (750 ml) chicken stock

1 garlic clove, crushed

salt and pepper

1 Put the beans in a large pot. Cover with fresh water, bring to the boil and boil 10 minutes. Reduce the heat and simmer 30 minutes, then drain.

2 Meanwhile, heat the oil in another large pot. Add the lamb cubes and fry until browned all over. Remove the lamb with a slotted spoon and reserve until needed.

3 ▼ Add the onion to the hot oil and cook until softened, about 5 minutes.

4 ▲ Return the lamb cubes to the pot and add the drained beans, bay leaf, stock, garlic and salt and pepper to taste. Bring to the boil. Reduce the heat, cover and simmer 1¼ hours, or until the lamb and beans are tender.

5 Discard the bay leaf and adjust the seasoning before serving.

Lamb Chops with Basil Sauce (top), Lamb and Bean Stew

Special Lamb Chops

SERVES 4

8 lamb rib chops
salt and pepper
1 egg
1 tsp Dijon mustard
3 tbsp fine dry breadcrumbs
3 tbsp sesame seeds
2 tbsp plain flour
1 oz (30 g) butter or margarine
1 tbsp vegetable oil

1 ▼ If necessary, trim any excess fat from the chops. With a small knife, scrape all the meat and fat off the top 2 in (5 cm) of the bone in each chop. Sprinkle the chops generously with salt and pepper.

2 ▲ In a bowl, beat the egg and mustard together. Pour into a shallow dish. In another dish, mix the breadcrumbs and sesame seeds. Place the flour in a third dish.

3 ▲ Coat each chop with flour, shaking off any excess. Dip in the egg and mustard mixture and then coat with the breadcrumb mixture, pressing it on the meat to get an even coating. Refrigerate 15 minutes.

4 ▲ Heat the butter or margarine and oil in a frying pan. Add the chops and fry over medium heat until crisp and golden and cooked to taste, 4–5 minutes on each side, turning gently with tongs.

Roast Rack of Lamb

2 racks of lamb, each with 8 chops, ends of bones scraped clean

3 tbsp Dijon mustard

1½ tbsp chopped fresh rosemary, or 1 tbsp dried rosemary

salt and pepper

2 oz (55 g) fine dry breadcrumbs

3 tbsp chopped fresh parsley

4 garlic cloves, crushed

2 fl oz (65 ml) olive oil

4 oz (115 g) butter or margarine

8 fl oz (250 ml) chicken stock

1 Preheat a 425°F/220°C/Gas 7 oven.

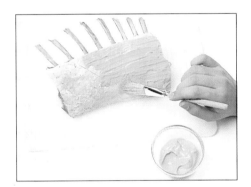

2 ▲ Brush the meaty side of the racks with the mustard. Sprinkle with the rosemary, salt and pepper.

3 ▲ In a bowl, mix the breadcrumbs with the parsley, garlic and half of the olive oil. Press this mixture evenly over the mustard on the racks of lamb. Wrap the scraped bone ends with foil. Put the racks in a roasting tin.

4 In a small saucepan, melt half the butter or margarine. Stir in the remaining olive oil. Drizzle this mixture over the racks of lamb.

5 Roast the racks of lamb, allowing 40 minutes for medium-rare meat and 50 minutes for medium.

6 Transfer the racks to a warmed serving platter, arranging them so the scraped ends of the bones are interlocked. Cover loosely with foil and set aside.

7 Pour the stock into the roasting tin and bring to the boil, scraping the bottom of the tin with a wooden spoon to mix in all the cooking juices. Remove from the heat and swirl in the remaining butter or margarine. Pour the gravy into a warmed sauceboat.

8 To serve, carve each rack by cutting down between the chop bones, or cut down after every 2 bones for double chops.

Lamb Kebabs

SERVES 4

1 lb (450 g) boned leg of lamb, cut into 1 in (2.5 cm) cubes

3 medium courgettes, cut into ½ in (1 cm) slices

3 tbsp mint jelly

2 tbsp fresh lemon juice

2 tbsp olive oil

1 tbsp chopped fresh mint

~ **VARIATION** ~

Substitute an equal quantity of orange marmalade for the mint jelly. Instead of fresh mint, use 2 teaspoons of grated orange rind.

1 Preheat the grill.

2 Thread the cubes of lamb and slices of courgette alternately onto metal or wooden skewers.

3 ▲ Combine the mint jelly, lemon juice, olive oil and chopped mint in a small saucepan. Stir over low heat until the jelly melts.

4 ▼ Brush the lamb and courgettes with the mint glaze. Lay them on the rack in the grill pan.

5 Cook under the grill, about 3 in (8 cm) from the heat, until browned and cooked to taste, 10–12 minutes, turning the skewers frequently. Serve on a bed of rice, if wished.

Lamb Burgers with Cucumber and Mint

SERVES 4

1½ lb (700 g) minced lamb

1 medium onion, finely chopped

1 tbsp paprika

2 tbsp chopped fresh parsley

2 tbsp chopped fresh mint, or 1 tbsp dried mint

salt and pepper

4 hamburger buns with sesame seeds, split open

FOR THE RELISH

1 large cucumber, thinly sliced

1 small red onion, thinly sliced

3 tbsp fresh lime or lemon juice

2 tbsp vegetable oil

4 tbsp chopped fresh mint, or 2 tbsp dried mint

2 spring onions, finely chopped

1 To make the relish, combine the cucumber, red onion, lime or lemon juice, oil, mint and spring onions in a non-metallic bowl. Cover the mixture and refrigerate at least 2 hours.

2 ▲ In a bowl, combine the lamb, onion, paprika, parsley, mint and a little salt and pepper. Mix thoroughly.

3 Preheat the grill.

4 ▲ Divide the lamb mixture into 4 equal portions and shape each into a burger 1 in (2.5 cm) thick.

5 Grill the burgers, about 3 in (8 cm) from the heat, allowing 5 minutes on each side for medium and 8 minutes on each side for well-done. At the same time, toast the cut surfaces of the buns briefly under the grill.

6 Serve the lamb burgers in the buns, with the cucumber and mint relish.

Lamb Kebabs (top), Lamb Burgers with Cucumber and Mint

Chicken Breasts with Prunes and Almonds

SERVES 4

1 oz (30 g) butter or margarine

1 tbsp vegetable oil

about 2½ lb (1.2 kg) chicken breast halves

1¼ pt (750 ml) chicken stock

4 oz (115 g) raisins

1 tbsp fresh thyme, or 1 tsp dried thyme

3 fresh sage leaves, chopped

3 tbsp chopped fresh parsley

1 tbsp chopped fresh marjoram, or 1 tsp dried marjoram

2 oz (55 g) fresh breadcrumbs

2 oz (55 g) ground almonds

12 prunes, stoned

4–6 whole cloves

½ tsp ground mace

pinch of saffron strands, crumbled

salt and pepper

1½ oz (45 g) flaked almonds, toasted

1 ▼ Melt the butter or margarine with the oil in a frying pan. Add the chicken and brown 10 minutes, turning once. Transfer the chicken pieces to a large pot.

~ COOK'S TIP ~

For ground almonds, chop whole or flaked almonds in a food processor until powdery.

2 ▲ Pour the stock into the pot and bring to the boil. Add all the remaining ingredients, except the toasted almonds, and stir well to mix. Simmer 45 minutes.

3 ▲ With tongs, remove the chicken from the pot and let cool. Bring the cooking liquid back to the boil and boil until well reduced, about 10 minutes, stirring frequently.

4 ▲ Remove the bones from the chicken and return the meat to the sauce. Heat through. Serve sprinkled with the toasted almonds.

Spicy Fried Chicken

SERVES 4

4 fl oz (125 ml) buttermilk
3 lb (1.35 kg) chicken pieces
vegetable oil, for frying
2 oz (55 g) plain flour
1 tbsp paprika
¼ tsp pepper
1 tbsp water

1 ▼ Pour the buttermilk into a large bowl and add the chicken pieces. Stir to coat, then set aside for 5 minutes.

2 Heat ¼ in (5 mm) of oil in a large frying pan over medium-high heat. Do not let the oil overheat.

3 ▲ In a bowl or plastic bag, combine the flour, paprika and pepper. One by one, lift the chicken pieces out of the buttermilk and dip into the flour to coat all over, shaking off any excess.

4 ▼ Add the chicken pieces to the hot oil and fry until lightly browned, about 10 minutes, turning over halfway through cooking time.

5 ▲ Reduce the heat to low and add the water to the frying pan. Cover and cook 30 minutes, turning the pieces over at 10-minute intervals. Uncover the pan and continue cooking until the chicken is very tender and the coating is crisp, about 15 minutes, turning every 5 minutes. Serve hot.

Roast Chicken

SERVES 4

1 × 3½ lb (1.6 kg) chicken
2 tbsp clear honey
1 tbsp brandy
1½ tbsp plain flour
5 fl oz (165 ml) chicken stock
FOR THE STUFFING
2 shallots or 1 small onion, chopped
4 rashers of bacon, chopped
1½ oz (45 g) button mushrooms, diced
1 tbsp butter or margarine
2 thick slices of white bread, diced
1 tbsp chopped fresh parsley
salt and pepper

1 ▼ For the stuffing, gently fry the shallots, bacon and mushrooms in a frying pan for 5 minutes. With a slotted spoon, transfer them to a bowl.

2 Pour off all but 2 tablespoons of bacon fat from the pan. Add the butter or margarine to the pan and fry the bread until golden brown. Add the bread to the bacon mixture. Stir in the parsley and salt and pepper to taste. Let cool.

3 Preheat a 350°F/180°C/Gas 4 oven.

4 ▲ Pack the stuffing into the body cavity of the chicken. Truss it with string, or secure with small skewers, to keep it in a neat shape.

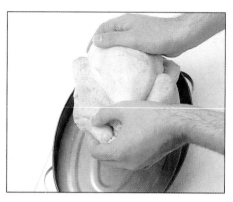

5 ▲ Transfer the chicken to a roasting tin which just holds it comfortably.

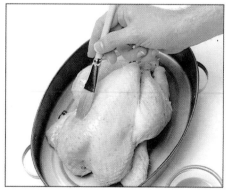

6 ▲ Mix the honey with the brandy. Brush half of the mixture over the chicken. Roast until the chicken is thoroughly cooked, about 1 hour 20 minutes. Baste the chicken frequently with the remaining honey mixture during roasting.

7 ▲ Transfer the chicken to a warmed serving platter. Cover with foil and set aside.

8 ▲ Strain the cooking juices into a measuring jug. Set aside to let the fat rise to the surface then skim it off.

9 ▲ Stir the flour into the sediments in the roasting tin. Add the skimmed juices and the stock. Boil rapidly until the gravy has thickened, stirring constantly.

10 Pour the gravy into a warmed sauceboat and serve with the chicken.

Chicken and Bacon Rolls

SERVES 4

16 rashers of bacon

8 chicken thighs, skin removed

FOR THE MARINADE

finely grated rind and juice of 1 orange

finely grated rind and juice of 1 lime or lemon

5 garlic cloves, crushed

1 tbsp chilli powder

1 tbsp paprika

1 tsp ground cumin

½ tsp dried oregano

1 tbsp olive oil

1 For the marinade, combine the citrus rind and juice, garlic, chilli powder, paprika, cumin, oregano and olive oil in a bowl.

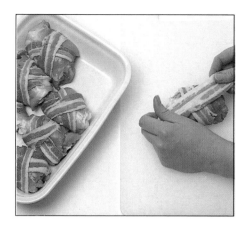

2 ▲ Wrap 2 rashers of bacon around each chicken thigh in a cross shape. Secure with wooden cocktail sticks. Arrange the wrapped chicken thighs in a baking dish.

3 Pour the marinade over the chicken, cover, and let marinate 1 hour at room temperature or several hours in the refrigerator.

4 Preheat a 375°F/190°C/Gas 5 oven.

5 ▼ Put the baking dish in the oven and bake until the chicken is cooked through and the bacon is crisp, about 40 minutes for small thighs and 1 hour for large thighs. Skim excess fat from the sauce before serving. Rice is a good accompaniment because there is plenty of sauce.

Hot and Spicy Chicken Drumsticks

SERVES 4

2 tbsp vegetable oil

8 chicken drumsticks, about 3 lb (1.35 kg)

1 medium onion, chopped

4 fl oz (125 ml) water

3 tbsp Dijon mustard

1 tbsp grated horseradish

1 tbsp Worcestershire sauce

1 tsp light brown sugar

¼ tsp salt

parsley sprigs, for garnishing

1 Heat the oil in a frying pan. Add the chicken drumsticks and brown them on all sides. With a spatula or tongs, remove the drumsticks from the pan and drain on kitchen paper.

2 ▲ Add the onion to the hot oil and cook until softened, about 5 minutes. Return the chicken to the pan. Stir in the water, mustard, horseradish, Worcestershire sauce, brown sugar and salt, and bring to the boil.

3 Reduce the heat to low. Cover the pan and simmer until the chicken is very tender, about 45 minutes, stirring occasionally.

4 ▼ Transfer the drumsticks to a warmed serving dish. Skim any fat off the cooking juices. Pour the juices over the chicken. Garnish with parsley and serve.

Chicken and Bacon Rolls (top), Hot and Spicy Chicken Drumsticks

Baby Chickens with Cranberry Sauce

SERVES 4

4 poussins or spring chickens, with giblets, each about 1 lb (450 g)
1½ oz (45 g) butter or margarine
salt and pepper
1 onion, quartered
2 fl oz (65 ml) port
5½ fl oz (170 ml) chicken stock
2 tbsp honey
5 oz (140 g) fresh cranberries

~ COOK'S TIP ~

If fresh cranberries are not available, use bottled cranberry sauce and omit the honey.

1 Preheat a 450°F/230°C/Gas 8 oven.

2 ▼ Smear the chickens on all sides with 1 oz (30 g) of the butter or margarine. Arrange them, on their sides, in a roasting tin in which they will fit comfortably. Sprinkle them with salt and pepper. Add the onion quarters to the tin. Chop the giblets and livers and arrange them around the chickens.

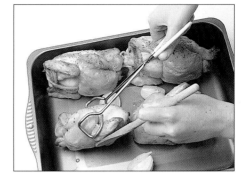

3 ▲ Roast 20 minutes, basting often with the melted fat in the tin. Turn the chickens onto their other sides and roast 20 minutes longer, basting often. Turn them breast up and continue roasting until they are cooked through, about 15 minutes. Transfer to a warmed serving dish. Cover with foil and set aside.

4 Skim any fat off the juices in the roasting tin. Put the tin on top of the stove and bring the juices to the boil. Add the port and bring back to the boil, stirring well to dislodge any particles sticking to the bottom of the tin.

5 ▲ Strain the sauce into a small saucepan. Add the stock, bring to the boil, and boil until reduced by half. Stir in the honey and cranberries. Simmer until the cranberries pop, about 3 minutes.

6 Remove the pan from the heat and swirl in the remaining butter or margarine. Season to taste, pour the sauce into a sauceboat and serve with the chickens.

Barbecued Chicken

SERVES 4

3 tbsp vegetable oil
1 large onion, chopped
6 fl oz (175 ml) tomato ketchup
6 fl oz (175 ml) water
2½ tbsp fresh lemon juice
1½ tbsp grated horseradish
1 tbsp light brown sugar
1 tbsp French mustard
3 lb (1.35 kg) chicken pieces

1 Preheat a 350°F/180°C/Gas 4 oven.

2 ▲ Heat 1 tablespoon of the oil in a saucepan. Add the onion and cook until softened, about 5 minutes. Stir in the ketchup, water, lemon juice, horseradish, brown sugar and mustard and bring to the boil. Reduce the heat and simmer the sauce 10 minutes, stirring occasionally.

3 ▲ Heat the remaining oil in a heavy frying pan. Add the chicken pieces and brown on all sides. Drain the chicken pieces on kitchen paper.

4 ▼ Transfer the chicken pieces to an 11 × 9 in (28 × 23 cm) baking dish and pour the sauce over the top.

5 ▲ Bake until the chicken is cooked and tender, about 1¼ hours, basting occasionally. Alternatively, barbecue over a medium heat for 40–50 minutes, turning once and brushing frequently with the sauce.

Traditional Chicken Pie

SERVES 6

2 oz (55 g) butter or margarine

1 medium onion, chopped

3 carrots, cut into ½ in (1 cm) dice

1 parsnip, cut into ½ in (1 cm) dice

3 tbsp plain flour

12 fl oz (350 ml) chicken stock

3 fl oz (85 ml) medium sherry

3 fl oz (85 ml) dry white wine

6 fl oz (175 ml) whipping cream

3½ oz (100 g) frozen peas, thawed

12 oz (350 g) cooked chicken meat, in chunks

1 tsp dried thyme

1 tbsp finely chopped fresh parsley

salt and pepper

FOR THE PASTRY

5½ oz (165 g) plain flour

½ tsp salt

4 oz (115 g) lard or vegetable fat

2–3 tbsp iced water

1 egg

2 tbsp milk

1 ▲ For the pastry, sift the flour and salt into a mixing bowl. Using a pastry blender, cut in the fat until the mixture resembles coarse breadcrumbs. Sprinkle in the water, 1 tablespoon at a time, tossing lightly with a fork until the dough forms a ball. Dust with flour, wrap and refrigerate until required.

2 Preheat a 400°F/200°C/Gas 6 oven.

3 ▲ Heat half of the butter or margarine in a saucepan. Add the onion, carrots and parsnip and cook until softened, about 10 minutes. Remove the vegetables from the pan with a slotted spoon.

4 ▲ Melt the remaining butter or margarine in the saucepan. Add the flour and cook 5 minutes, stirring constantly. Stir in the stock, sherry and white wine. Bring the sauce to the boil, and continue boiling for 1 minute, stirring constantly.

5 ▲ Add the cream, peas, chicken, thyme and parsley to the sauce. Season to taste with salt and pepper. Simmer 1 minute, stirring.

6 ▼ Transfer the chicken mixture to a 3½ pt (2 litre) shallow baking dish.

7 On a lightly floured surface, roll out the pastry to ½ in (1 cm) thickness. Lay the pastry over the baking dish and trim off the excess. Dampen the rim of the dish. With a fork, press the pastry to the rim to seal.

8 Cut decorative shapes from the pastry trimmings.

9 ▲ Lightly whisk the egg with the milk. Brush the pastry all over with the egg wash. Arrange the pastry shapes in an attractive design on top. Brush again with the egg wash. Make 1 or 2 holes in the crust so steam can escape during baking.

10 Bake the pie until the pastry is golden brown, about 35 minutes. Serve hot.

Chicken with Sweet Potatoes

SERVES 6

grated rind and juice of 1 large navel orange

3 fl oz (85 ml) soy sauce

1 in (2.5 cm) piece of fresh root ginger, peeled and finely grated

¼ tsp pepper

2½ lb (1.2 kg) chicken pieces

2 oz (55 g) flour

3 tbsp corn oil

1 oz (30 g) butter or margarine

2 lb (900 g) sweet potatoes, peeled and cut into 1 in (2.5 cm) pieces

1½ oz (45 g) light brown sugar

1 ▲ In a plastic bag, combine the orange rind and juice, soy sauce, root ginger and pepper. Add the chicken pieces. Put the bag in a mixing bowl (this will keep the chicken immersed in the marinade), and seal. Let marinate in the refrigerator overnight.

2 Preheat a 425°F/220°C/gas 7 oven.

3 ▼ Drain the chicken, reserving the marinade. Coat the pieces with flour, shaking off any excess.

4 Heat 2 tablespoons of the oil in a frying pan. Add the chicken pieces and brown on all sides. Drain.

5 Put the remaining oil and the butter or margarine in a 12 × 9 in (30 × 23 cm) baking dish. Heat in the oven for a few minutes.

6 ▲ Put the potato pieces in the bottom of the dish, tossing well to coat with the butter and oil. Arrange the chicken pieces in a single layer on top of the potatoes. Cover with foil and bake for 40 minutes.

7 Mix the reserved marinade with the brown sugar. Remove the foil from the baking dish and pour the marinade mixture over the chicken and potatoes. Bake uncovered until the chicken and potatoes are cooked through and tender, about 20 minutes.

Mexican Chicken

SERVES 4

1 × 3 lb (1.35 kg) chicken
1 tsp salt
12 taco shells
1 small head of iceberg lettuce, shredded
6 oz (170 g) tomatoes, chopped
8 fl oz (250 ml) soured cream
4 oz (115 g) Cheddar cheese, grated

FOR THE SAUCE

8 fl oz (250 ml) fresh tomatoes, skinned, cooked and sieved
1–2 garlic cloves, crushed
½ tsp cider vinegar
½ tsp dried oregano
½ tsp ground cumin
1–2 tbsp mild chilli powder

1 Put the chicken in a large pot and add the salt and enough water to cover. Bring to the boil. Reduce the heat and simmer until the chicken is thoroughly cooked, about 45 minutes. Remove the chicken and let cool. Reserve 4 fl oz (125 ml) of the chicken stock for the sauce.

2 ▲ Remove the chicken meat from the bones, discarding all skin. Chop the meat coarsely.

3 For the sauce, combine all the ingredients with the stock in a saucepan and bring to the boil. Stir in the chicken meat. Simmer until the sauce thickens considerably, about 20 minutes, stirring occasionally.

4 Preheat a 350°F/180°C/Gas 4 oven.

5 ▲ Spread out the taco shells on 2 baking trays. Heat in the oven for 7 minutes.

6 Meanwhile, put the shredded lettuce, chopped tomatoes, soured cream and grated cheese in individual serving dishes.

7 ▲ To serve, spoon a little of the chicken mixture into each taco shell. Garnish with the lettuce, tomatoes, soured cream and cheese.

Roast Turkey with Middle-Eastern Stuffing

SERVES 12

1 12 lb (5.5 kg) turkey, with giblets
6 oz (170 g) softened butter
salt and pepper
1 lemon, quartered
2 onions, quartered
16 fl oz (500 ml) cold water
6 small aubergines (optional)
1 tbsp cornflour
parsley sprigs, for garnishing
FOR THE STUFFING
1 oz (30 g) pine kernels
6 oz (170 g) couscous
12 fl oz (375 ml) boiling water
1 oz (30 g) butter or margarine
6 spring onions, chopped
1 red pepper, seeded and chopped
1½ oz (45 g) raisins
½ tsp ground cumin
3 tbsp chopped fresh parsley
1 tbsp fresh lemon juice

1 Preheat a 325°F/165°C/gas 3 oven. Put the pine kernels on a baking sheet in the oven until golden brown, about 5–10 minutes, stirring occasionally.

2 For the stuffing, put the couscous into a large bowl and pour the boiling water over it. Let stand 10 minutes.

3 ▲ Add the pine kernels to the couscous with the rest of the stuffing ingredients. Mix with a fork to keep the grains of couscous separate.

4 Rinse the turkey inside and out with cold water. Pat dry. Gently slide your hand under the breast skin and loosen it from the meat.

5 ▲ Spread two-thirds of the softened butter under the skin all over the breast meat.

6 Fill the neck end of the turkey with stuffing, without packing it down. Reserve any remaining stuffing to serve separately. Sew the neck flap with a trussing needle and thread, or secure with poultry pins.

7 ▲ Sprinkle the body cavity with salt and pepper. Put the quartered lemon and one of the onions inside. Tie the legs together with string.

8 Smear the remaining butter all over the turkey. Wrap it loosely in foil and set in a roasting pan. Roast, allowing 25 minutes per pound (55 minutes per kg). Remove the foil for the last 30 minutes of roasting. To test if cooked, pierce the thigh with the tip of a sharp knife; the juices that run out should be clear.

9 ▲ Meanwhile, put the giblets in a saucepan with the remaining onion and the water. Bring to a boil, simmer 1 hour, then strain.

10 If using, halve the aubergines and steam until tender, about 10 minutes. Scoop out the inside, leaving a thick shell, and fill with the remaining stuffing. Alternatively, serve the remaining stuffing separately.

11 When the turkey is done, transfer it to a warmed serving platter. Cover with foil and let rest 30 minutes.

12 ▲ Skim the fat off the drippings in the roasting pan. Stir the cornflour into a little of the giblet stock until smooth. Add the remaining giblet stock to the roasting pan, then stir in the cornflour mixture. Bring to the boil, scraping the bottom of the pan well with a wooden spoon. Simmer 15 minutes. Strain the gravy and adjust the seasoning.

13 Garnish the turkey with the stuffed aubergines, if using, and parsley sprigs, and serve the gravy in a warmed sauceboat.

Hot Turkey Sandwich

SERVES 4

2 oz (55 g) butter or margarine

½ small onion, finely chopped

8 oz (225 g) button mushrooms, quartered

1¼ lb (575 g) roast turkey breast

4 thick slices of wholewheat bread

16 fl oz (450 ml) thick turkey gravy

parsley sprigs, for garnishing

1 Melt half the butter or margarine in a frying pan. Add the onion and cook until softened, about 5 minutes.

~ **VARIATION** ~

If preferred, the sandwich bread may be toasted and buttered.

2 Add the mushrooms and cook until the moisture they render has evaporated, about 5 minutes, stirring occasionally.

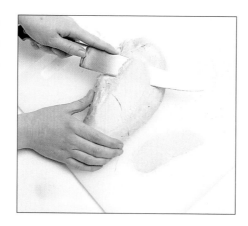

3 ▲ Meanwhile, skin the turkey breast, and carve into 4 thick slices.

4 In a saucepan, reheat the turkey gravy. Stir in the onion and mushroom mixture.

5 ▲ Spread the slices of bread with the remaining butter or margarine. Set a slice on each of 4 plates and top with the turkey slices. Pour the mushroom gravy over the turkey and serve hot, garnished with parsley.

Leftover Turkey Casserole

SERVES 6

4 fl oz (125 ml) vegetable oil

4 eggs

16 fl oz (450 ml) milk

4 oz (115 g) plain flour

salt and pepper

1½ lb (700 g) cooked turkey meat, cubed

4 fl oz (125 ml) thick plain yoghurt

3 oz (85 g) cornflakes, crushed

1 Preheat a 425°F/220°C/Gas 7 oven.

2 Pour the oil into a 13 × 9 in (33 × 23 cm) baking dish. Heat in the oven about 10 minutes.

3 Meanwhile, beat the eggs in a mixing bowl. Add the milk. Sift in the flour and add a little salt and pepper. Mix until the batter is smooth. Set aside.

4 ▲ Coat the turkey cubes in the yoghurt, then roll in the crushed cornflakes to coat all over.

5 ▲ Remove the baking dish from the oven and pour in the prepared batter. Arrange the turkey pieces on top. Return to the oven and bake until the batter is set and golden, 35–40 minutes. Serve hot.

Hot Turkey Sandwich (top), Leftover Turkey Casserole

Turkey Kiev

4 turkey cutlets (boneless slices of breast), each about 6 oz (175 g)

salt and pepper

4 oz (115 g) butter or margarine, chilled

1 tsp grated orange rind

2 tbsp chopped fresh chives

plain flour, for dredging

3 eggs, beaten

4 oz (115 g) fine dry breadcrumbs

vegetable oil, for frying

orange wedges and parsley, for garnishing

1 ▼ Place each cutlet between 2 sheets of greaseproof paper. With the flat side of a meat mallet, beat until about ¼ in (5 mm) thick, being careful not to split the meat. Remove the greaseproof paper. Sprinkle the cutlets with salt and pepper.

2 ▲ Cut the butter or margarine into 4 finger-shaped pieces. Place a piece crosswise in the middle of a cutlet. Sprinkle with a little orange rind and chives.

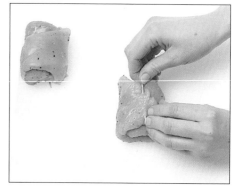

3 ▲ Fold in the 2 long sides of the cutlet, then roll up from a short end. Secure with wooden cocktail sticks. Repeat with the remaining cutlets.

4 Dredge each roll lightly with flour, shaking off any excess. Dip in the beaten eggs, then roll in the breadcrumbs to coat evenly. Refrigerate 1 hour to set the breadcrumb coating.

5 Pour enough oil into a frying pan to make a ½ in (1 cm) layer and heat. Add the breaded turkey rolls to the hot oil and fry until crisp and golden on all sides, 15–20 minutes, turning gently with tongs.

6 Remove the cocktail sticks before serving. Garnish with orange wedges and parsley.

Turkey Breasts with Lemon and Sage

SERVES 4

4 turkey cutlets (boneless slices of breast), each about 6 oz (175 g)

salt and pepper

1 tbsp grated lemon rind

1 tbsp chopped fresh sage, or 1 tsp dried sage

2 fl oz (65 ml) fresh lemon juice

6 tbsp vegetable oil

4 oz (115 g) fine dry breadcrumbs

fresh sage leaves, for garnishing

lemon slices, for garnishing

1 Place each cutlet between 2 sheets of greaseproof paper. With the flat side of a meat mallet, beat until about ¼ in (5 mm) thick, being careful not to split the meat. Remove the greaseproof paper. Sprinkle the cutlets with salt and pepper.

2 ▲ In a small bowl, combine the lemon rind, sage, lemon juice and 2 tablespoons of the oil. Stir well to mix.

~ **VARIATION** ~

For a delicious alternative, substitute fresh tarragon leaves for the sage.

3 ▼ Arrange the turkey cutlets, in one layer, in 1 or 2 shallow baking dishes. Divide the lemon mixture evenly between the dishes and rub well into the turkey. Let marinate 20 minutes.

4 ▲ Heat the remaining oil in a frying pan. Dredge the turkey breasts in the breadcrumbs, shaking off the excess. Fry in the hot oil until golden brown, about 2 minutes on each side. Serve garnished with sage leaves and lemon slices.

Turkey Chilli

SERVES 8

2 tbsp vegetable oil

1 medium onion, halved and thinly sliced

1 green pepper, seeded and diced

3 garlic cloves, crushed

2 lb (900 g) minced turkey

2–3 tbsp mild chilli powder

1½ tsp ground cumin

1 tsp dried oregano

1 × 16 oz (450 g) can chopped tomatoes

2 tbsp tomato purée

8 fl oz (250 ml) chicken stock

1 × 16 oz (450 g) can red kidney beans, drained and rinsed

¼ tsp salt

1 Heat the oil in a large saucepan over a medium heat. Add the onion, green pepper and garlic and cook until softened, about 5 minutes, stirring frequently.

2 ▼ Add the turkey and cook until it is lightly browned, about 5 minutes longer, stirring to break up the meat.

3 ▼ Stir in the chilli powder, cumin and oregano. Add the tomatoes, tomato purée, chicken stock, kidney beans and salt, and stir well.

4 Bring to the boil, then reduce the heat and simmer 30 minutes, stirring occasionally. Serve the chilli with boiled rice.

Turkey and Pasta Bake

SERVES 4

2½ oz (70 g) butter or margarine

8 oz (225 g) mushrooms, thinly sliced

1 oz (30 g) plain flour

14 fl oz (400 ml) milk

16 fl oz (450 ml) chicken stock

2 fl oz (65 ml) dry white wine

10 oz (300 g) spaghetti

12 oz (350 g) chopped cooked turkey meat

5 oz (140 g) frozen peas, thawed and drained

2½ oz (70 g) Parmesan cheese, freshly grated

salt and pepper

1 oz (30 g) fine fresh breadcrumbs

1 Preheat a 375°F/190°C/Gas 5 oven. Grease a shallow 5 pt (3 litre) baking dish.

2 ▲ Melt 2 oz (55 g) of the butter or margarine in a medium saucepan. Add the mushrooms and cook 5 minutes, stirring frequently. Stir in the flour and cook 3 minutes, stirring constantly. Pour in the milk, stock and white wine and bring to the boil, stirring. Reduce the heat and simmer 5 minutes.

3 Meanwhile, cook the spaghetti in a large pan of boiling salted water until just tender (see pack instructions for suggested cooking time). Drain.

4 ▼ Transfer the spaghetti to a mixing bowl. Pour in the mushroom sauce and mix well. Stir in the turkey, peas, half of the Parmesan and salt and pepper to taste. Transfer the mixture to the baking dish.

5 In a small bowl, combine the remaining Parmesan with the breadcrumbs. Sprinkle evenly over the turkey mixture. Dot with the remaining butter or margarine, cut into pieces. Bake until bubbling and golden, 30–40 minutes. Serve hot, in the baking dish.

Turkey Chilli (top), Turkey and Pasta Bake

PASTA, PIZZA & GRAINS

~

Versatile pasta and grains – rice, couscous, and bulgur wheat – star in the recipes here, with a myriad of tasty sauces and flavourings, for first courses or main dishes. And there are pizzas with mouthwatering toppings.

Spicy Cheese Lasagne

SERVES 8

8 oz (225 g) lasagne

2 oz (55 g) butter or margarine

1 large onion, finely chopped

3 garlic cloves, crushed

1½ tbsp chopped green chilli pepper

2 oz (55 g) plain flour

1¾ pt (1 litre) milk

1¼ pt (750 ml) canned chopped
    tomatoes

1 large courgette, sliced

½ tsp crushed dried chilli pepper

salt and pepper

12 oz (350 g) Cheddar cheese, grated

1 Preheat a 375°F/190°C/Gas 5 oven.
Grease a 13 × 9 in (33 × 23 cm) dish.

2 Put the lasagne sheets, one at a
time, in a bowl of hot water, and let
soak for 10–15 minutes.

3 ▲ Melt the butter or margarine in
a large saucepan. Add the onion,
garlic and chopped chilli and cook
until softened, about 5 minutes.

4 Stir in the flour and cook 3
minutes, stirring constantly. Pour in
the milk and bring to the boil,
stirring. Reduce the heat to low and
simmer gently until thickened, about
5 minutes, stirring occasionally.

5 Stir the tomatoes, courgettes, and
dried chilli pepper into the sauce.
Season with salt and pepper.

6 Spoon a little of the sauce into the
prepared baking dish and spread it out
evenly over the bottom. Cover with a
layer of lasagne.

7 ▲ Add one-third of the remaining
sauce and one-third of the cheese.
Repeat the layers until all the
ingredients are used.

8 Bake until the top is golden and
bubbling, about 45 minutes. Serve
hot, in the dish.

Spaghetti with Rich Tomato Sauce

SERVES 4

12 oz (350 g) spaghetti

4 garlic cloves, crushed

10–15 sun-dried tomatoes preserved in
    oil, drained and chopped

5 oz (140 g) black olives, stoned

4 fl oz (125 ml) extra-virgin olive oil

3 beef tomatoes, peeled, seeded and
    chopped

3 tbsp capers, drained

3 tbsp chopped fresh basil, plus leaves
    for garnishing, or 1 tsp dried basil

salt and pepper

1 Cook the spaghetti in a large pan of
boiling salted water until just tender
to the bite (check packet instructions
for timing). Drain well.

2 ▲ In a food processor or blender,
combine the garlic, sun-dried
tomatoes and half the olives. Process
until finely chopped.

3 With the motor running, slowly
add the olive oil. Continue processing
until thickened.

4 ▼ Transfer the mixture to a mixing
bowl. Stir in the fresh tomatoes,
capers and basil. Season with salt and
pepper to taste.

5 Return the spaghetti to the
saucepan and add the tomato sauce.
Toss well. Serve immediately,
garnished with the remaining olives
and fresh basil leaves, if wished

Spicy Cheese Lasagne (top), Spaghetti with Rich Tomato Sauce

Pasta with Fresh Basil Sauce

SERVES 4

about 2 oz (55 g) chopped fresh basil

about 1 oz (30 g) chopped fresh parsley

1½ oz (45 g) Parmesan cheese, freshly grated

2 garlic cloves

2 oz (55 g) butter or margarine, at room temperature

2 fl oz (65 ml) extra-virgin olive oil

salt

12 oz (350 g) mixed green and white fettucine or tagliatelle

2 oz (55 g) pine kernels, toasted

fresh basil leaves, for garnishing

1 ▲ In a food processor or blender, combine the basil, parsley, Parmesan and garlic. Process until finely chopped.

2 Add the butter or margarine and process to mix well.

3 ▼ With the machine running, slowly add the olive oil. Season with salt to taste.

4 Cook the pasta in a large pan of boiling salted water until just tender (check packet instructions for timing). Drain well.

5 Toss the hot pasta with the basil sauce. Sprinkle with the pine kernels, garnish with basil and serve.

Pasta Quills with Cheesy Aubergine Sauce

SERVES 6

1¼ lb (575 g) aubergine, cut into ½ in (1 cm) cubes

salt and pepper

3 tbsp olive oil

½ oz (15 g) butter or margarine

1 garlic clove, chopped

16 fl oz (450 ml) canned chopped tomatoes

12 oz (350 g) pasta quills (penne)

4 oz (115 g) firm goat cheese, cubed

3 tbsp shredded fresh basil, or 1 tsp dried basil

1 Put the aubergine cubes in a large colander and sprinkle them lightly with salt. Let drain at least 30 minutes.

2 Rinse the aubergine under cold water and drain well. Dry on kitchen paper.

3 Heat the oil and butter or margarine in a large saucepan. Add the aubergine and fry until just golden on all sides, stirring frequently.

4 ▲ Stir in the garlic and tomatoes. Simmer until thickened, about 15 minutes. Season with salt and pepper.

5 ▲ Cook the pasta quills in a large pan of boiling salted water until just tender (check packet instructions for timing). Drain well and transfer to a warmed serving bowl.

6 Add the aubergine sauce, goat cheese and basil to the pasta and toss well together. Serve immediately.

Pasta with Fresh Basil Sauce (top), Pasta Quills with Cheesy Aubergine Sauce

Pasta with Chicken and Sausage Sauce

SERVES 4

3 tbsp olive oil

1 lb (450 g) skinless boneless chicken
breasts, cut into ½ in (1 cm) pieces

3 small spicy cooked sausages, cut
diagonally into ½ in (1 cm) slices

salt and pepper

6 spring onions, cut diagonally into ¼ in
(5 mm) lengths

10 sun-dried tomatoes preserved in oil,
drained and chopped

8 fl oz (250 ml) canned chopped
tomatoes

1 medium-sized courgette, cut
diagonally into ¼ in (5 mm) slices

12 oz (350 g) bow-tie pasta (farfalle)

1 ▼ Heat the olive oil in a frying
pan. Add the chicken and sausage
pieces with a little salt and pepper and
cook until browned, about 10
minutes. With a slotted spoon,
remove the chicken and sausage from
the pan and drain on kitchen paper.

2 ▲ Add the spring onions and sun-
dried tomatoes to the pan and cook
until softened, about 5 minutes.

3 ▲ Stir in the canned tomatoes and
cook until thickened, about 5
minutes.

4 ▲ Add the courgette and return
the chicken and sausage to the pan.
Cook 5 minutes longer.

5 Cook the pasta in a large pan of
boiling salted water until just tender
(check packet instructions for
timing). Drain well.

6 Serve the pasta with the chicken
and sausage sauce.

Pasta with Spinach, Bacon and Mushrooms

SERVES 4

6 rashers of bacon, cut in small pieces
½ small onion, finely chopped
8 oz (225 g) small mushrooms, quartered
1 lb (450 g) fresh spinach leaves, stems removed
¼ tsp grated nutmeg
salt and pepper
12 oz (350 g) pasta shells
2 tbsp freshly grated Parmesan cheese

1 ▼ In a frying pan, cook the bacon until it is browned and the fat is rendered. Drain the bacon on kitchen paper, then put it in a bowl.

2 Add the onion to the bacon fat in the pan and cook until softened, about 5 minutes.

3 ▲ Add the mushrooms to the pan and cook until lightly browned, about 5 minutes, stirring frequently. With a slotted spoon, transfer the onion and mushrooms to the bacon in the bowl. Pour off the bacon fat from the frying pan.

4 ▼ Add the spinach to the pan and cook over a medium heat until wilted, stirring constantly.

5 Sprinkle with the nutmeg. Raise the heat to high and cook briskly, stirring to evaporate excess liquid from the spinach. Transfer the spinach to a board and chop it coarsely. Return it to the pan.

6 ▲ Return the bacon, mushrooms and onion to the pan and stir to mix with the spinach. Season with salt and pepper. Set aside.

7 Cook the pasta in a large pan of boiling salted water until just tender (check packet instructions for timing). Just before the pasta is ready, reheat the spinach mixture.

8 Drain the pasta well and return to the saucepan. Add the spinach mixture and toss well to mix. Sprinkle with Parmesan cheese before serving.

Pasta Spirals with Spicy Sausage

SERVES 4

3 tbsp olive oil

1 lb (450 g) chorizo or other spicy cooked sausages, cut diagonally in ½ in (1 cm) slices

1 onion, chopped

1 garlic clove, crushed

2 red peppers, seeded and sliced

12 oz (350 g) drained canned sweetcorn, or frozen sweetcorn, thawed

salt and pepper

12 oz (350 g) pasta spirals (fusilli)

1 tbsp chopped fresh basil, or ½ tsp dried basil

fresh basil leaves, for garnishing

1 Heat 1 tablespoon of the oil in a frying pan. Add the sausage slices and brown them on both sides.

2 Remove the sausage from the pan with a slotted spoon and drain on kitchen paper.

3 ▲ Heat the remaining oil in the pan and add the onion, garlic and peppers. Cook until softened, about 5 minutes, stirring frequently.

4 ▲ Stir the sausage and sweetcorn into the pepper mixture and heat through, about 5 minutes. Season with salt and pepper.

5 Cook the pasta in boiling salted water until just tender (check packet instructions for timing). Drain well and return to the pan.

6 Add the sausage sauce and basil to the pasta. Toss together well, garnish with basil and serve immediately.

Pasta with Tomato and Lime Sauce

SERVES 4

1 lb (450 g) very ripe tomatoes, peeled and chopped

1 small bunch of tender, young rocket or spinach leaves

4 garlic cloves, crushed

grated rind of ½ lime

juice of 2 limes

¼ tsp chilli sauce

12 oz (350 g) thin spaghetti (capellini)

2 fl oz (65 ml) olive oil

salt and pepper

freshly grated Parmesan cheese, for serving

1 ▼ Combine the tomatoes, rocket, garlic, lime rind and juice and chilli sauce. Stir well to mix. Set aside for 20–30 minutes.

2 Cook the pasta in boiling salted water until just tender (check packet instructions for timing). Drain and return to the pan.

3 ▲ Add the olive oil and tomato and lime sauce to the pasta. Toss well together. Season with salt and pepper. Add Parmesan cheese to taste, toss again and serve.

Pasta Spirals with Spicy Sausage (top), Pasta with Tomato and Lime Sauce

Macaroni Cheese

SERVES 4

4 oz (115 g) macaroni

2 oz (55 g) butter or margarine

1 oz (30 g) plain flour

1 pt (575 ml) milk

6 oz (170 g) Cheddar cheese, grated

3 tbsp finely chopped fresh parsley

salt and pepper

3½ oz (100 g) dry breadcrumbs

1½ oz (45 g) Parmesan cheese, freshly grated

1 Preheat a 350°F/180°C/Gas 4 oven. Grease a 10 in (25 cm) gratin dish.

2 Cook the macaroni in boiling salted water until just tender (check packet instructions for timing). Drain well.

3 Melt the butter or margarine in a saucepan. Add the flour and cook 2 minutes, stirring. Stir in the milk. Bring to a boil, stirring constantly, and simmer until thickened, about 5 minutes.

4 ▲ Remove the pan from the heat. Add the macaroni, Cheddar cheese and parsley to the sauce and mix well. Season with salt and pepper.

5 Transfer the mixture to the prepared gratin dish, spreading it out evenly with a spoon.

6 ▲ Toss together the breadcrumbs and Parmesan cheese with a fork. Sprinkle over the macaroni.

7 Bake until the top is golden brown and the macaroni mixture is bubbling, 30–35 minutes.

Noodle and Vegetable Bake

SERVES 10

1 lb (450 g) egg noodles

3 oz (85 g) butter or margarine

1 onion, chopped

3 garlic cloves, chopped

3 carrots, grated

12 oz (350 g) small mushrooms, quartered

3 eggs, beaten

12 oz (350 g) cottage cheese

8 fl oz (250 ml) soured cream

2 courgettes, finely chopped in a food processor

3 tbsp chopped fresh basil, or 1 tbsp dried basil

salt and pepper

fresh basil leaves, for garnishing

1 Preheat a 350°F/180°C/Gas 4 oven. Grease a 13 × 9 in (33 × 23 cm) baking dish.

2 Cook the pasta in boiling salted water until just tender (check packet instructions for timing). Drain and rinse with cold water. Transfer to a mixing bowl.

3 Melt two-thirds of the butter or margarine in a frying pan. Add the onion, garlic and carrots and cook until tender, about 10 minutes, stirring frequently.

4 ▲ Stir in the mushrooms and cook 5 minutes longer. Add the vegetables to the noodles in the mixing bowl.

5 In a small bowl, combine the eggs, cottage cheese, soured cream, courgettes, basil and salt and pepper to taste. Mix well.

6 ▲ Add the cottage cheese mixture to the noodles and mix well. Transfer to the prepared baking dish. Dot the top with the remaining butter or margarine.

7 Cover the dish with foil. Bake until the casserole is set, about 1 hour. Serve hot, in the baking dish, garnished with basil leaves.

Macaroni Cheese (top), Noodle and Vegetable Bake

Baked Seafood Pasta

SERVES 6

8 oz (225 g) egg noodles

2½ oz (70 g) butter or margarine

1 oz (30 g) flour

16 fl oz (500 ml) milk

½ tsp mustard powder

1 tsp fresh lemon juice

1 tbsp tomato purée

salt and pepper

2 tbsp minced onion

2 oz (55 g) finely diced celery

4 oz (125 g) small mushrooms, sliced

8 oz (225 g) cooked peeled shrimps

8 oz (225 g) crab meat

1 tbsp chopped fresh dill

fresh dill sprigs, for garnishing

1 Preheat a 350°F/180°C/gas 4 oven. Generously butter a 3½ pt (2 litre) baking dish.

2 Cook the noodles in a large pan of boiling salted water until just tender to the bite (check packet instructions for timing). Drain well.

3 ▲ While the pasta is cooking, make a white sauce. Melt 1½ oz (45 g) of the butter or margarine in a saucepan. Add the flour and cook 2 minutes, stirring. Stir in the milk. Bring to the boil, stirring constantly, and simmer until thickened, about 5 minutes.

4 ▲ Add the mustard, lemon juice and tomato purée to the sauce and mix well. Season to taste with salt and pepper. Set aside.

5 ▲ Melt the remaining butter or margarine in a frying pan. Add the onion, celery and mushrooms. Cook until softened, about 5 minutes.

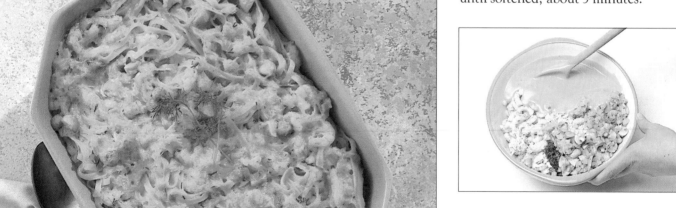

6 ▲ In a mixing bowl, combine the pasta, sauce, vegetables, shrimps, crab meat and dill. Stir well to mix.

7 Pour the mixture into the prepared baking dish. Bake until piping hot and the top is lightly browned, 30–40 minutes. Garnish with dill sprigs, if wished.

Pasta-Stuffed Peppers

SERVES 4

6 rashers of bacon, chopped

1 small onion, chopped

12 fl oz (350 ml) canned chopped tomatoes

⅛ tsp crushed dried chilli peppers

2 oz (55 g) macaroni

6 oz (170 g) Mozzarella cheese, diced

12 black olives, stoned and thinly sliced

salt and pepper

2 large red peppers

2 large yellow peppers

2 tbsp olive oil

1 Preheat a 350°F/180°C/Gas 4 oven. Grease an 8 in (20 cm) baking dish.

2 ▲ In a frying pan, cook the bacon until browned and the fat is rendered. Drain the bacon on kitchen paper.

3 Add the onion to the bacon fat in the pan and cook until softened, about 5 minutes. Pour off excess fat.

4 ▲ Stir in the tomatoes and dried chilli peppers. Cook over high heat until thickened, about 10 minutes.

5 Meanwhile, cook the pasta in a large pan of boiling salted water until just tender (check packet instructions for timing). Drain well.

6 ▲ Put the pasta in a mixing bowl and add the bacon, tomato sauce, Mozzarella cheese and olives. Toss well to mix. Season to taste.

7 Cut the stem end off each pepper; reserve these 'lids'. Remove the seeds from inside the peppers and cut out the white ribs.

8 ▲ Divide the pasta mixture evenly among the peppers. Put on the "lids". Brush the peppers all over with the olive oil and set them in the prepared baking dish.

9 Cover the dish with foil and bake 30 minutes. Remove the foil and bake until the peppers are tender, 25–30 minutes longer.

Broccoli and Goat Cheese Pizza

SERVES 2–3

8 oz (225 g) broccoli florets
2 tbsp cornmeal, or polenta
4 fl oz (125 ml) fresh tomatoes, skinned, cooked and sieved
6 cherry tomatoes, halved
12 black olives, stoned
4 oz (115 g) goat cheese, cut into pieces
1½ oz (45 g) Parmesan cheese, grated
1 tbsp olive oil
FOR THE PIZZA DOUGH
8–9 oz (225–250 g) plain flour
1 package active dry yeast (¼ oz/7.5 g)
⅛ tsp sugar
5 fl oz (150 ml) tepid water
2 tbsp olive oil
½ tsp salt

1 For the pizza dough, combine 3 oz (85 g) of the flour, the yeast and sugar in a food processor. With the motor running, pour in the water. Turn the motor off. Add the oil, 5 oz (140 g) of the remaining flour and the salt.

2 ▲ Process until a ball of dough is formed, adding more water, 1 teaspoon at a time, if the dough is too dry, or the remaining flour, 1 tablespoon at a time, if it is too wet.

3 ▲ Put the dough in an oiled bowl and turn it so the ball of dough is oiled all over. Cover the bowl and let the dough rise in a warm place until doubled in size, about 1 hour.

4 ▲ Meanwhile, cook the broccoli florets in boiling salted water or steam them until just tender, about 5 minutes. Drain well and set aside.

5 Preheat the oven to the highest setting. Oil a 12 in (30 cm) round pizza pan and sprinkle with the cornmeal.

6 When the dough has risen, turn out onto a lightly floured surface. Punch down the dough to deflate it, and knead it briefly.

~ COOK'S TIP ~

If more convenient, the pizza dough can be used as soon as it is made, without any rising.

7 ▲ Roll out the dough to a 12 in (30 cm) round. Lay the dough on the pizza pan and press it down evenly.

8 ▲ Spread the tomato sauce evenly onto the pizza base, leaving a rim of dough uncovered around the edge about ½ in (1 cm) wide.

9 ▲ Arrange the broccoli florets, tomatoes, and olives on the tomato sauce and sprinkle with the cheeses. Drizzle the olive oil over the top.

10 Bake until the cheese melts and the edge of the pizza base is puffed and browned, 10–15 minutes.

Pitta-Bread Pizzas

SERVES 4

4 × 6 in (15 cm) round pitta breads, split in half horizontally
2 fl oz (65 ml) olive oil
salt and pepper
1 small red pepper, seeded and sliced
1 small yellow pepper, seeded and sliced
8 oz (225 g) small red potatoes, cooked and sliced
1 tbsp chopped fresh rosemary, or 1 tsp dried rosemary
1½ oz (45 g) Parmesan cheese, freshly grated

1 Preheat a 350°F/180°C/Gas 4 oven.

2 ▼ Place the pitta rounds on a baking tray. Brush them on both sides with 2 tablespoons of the oil. Sprinkle with salt. Bake until pale golden and crisp, about 10 minutes.

3 ▲ Heat the remaining oil in a frying pan. Add the peppers and cook until softened, about 5 minutes, stirring frequently.

4 ▲ Add the potatoes and rosemary to the peppers. Heat through, about 3 minutes, stirring well. Season with salt and pepper.

5 Preheat the grill.

6 ▲ Divide the pepper-potato mixture between the pitta rounds. Sprinkle with the Parmesan cheese and transfer to the grill pan.

7 Grill about 3 in (8 cm) from the heat until golden, 3–4 minutes.

Onion, Olive and Anchovy Pizza

SERVES 4

6 tbsp olive oil

1 lb (450 g) onions, thinly sliced

3 garlic cloves, crushed

1 bay leaf

2 tsp dried thyme

salt and pepper

2 cans anchovy fillets, drained and blotted dry on kitchen paper

12 olives, mixed black and green

FOR THE PIZZA DOUGH

4 oz (115 g) wholewheat flour

3 oz (85 g) plain flour

1¼ tsp active dry yeast

⅛ tsp sugar

5 fl oz (150 ml) tepid water

2 tbsp olive oil

½ tsp salt

1 For the pizza dough, in a food processor combine the flours, yeast and sugar. With the motor running, pour in the tepid water. Turn the motor off. Add the oil and salt. Process until a ball of dough is formed.

2 Put the dough in an oiled bowl and turn it to coat with oil. Cover and let rise until doubled in size.

3 ▲ Heat 3 tablespoons of the oil in a frying pan. Add the onions, garlic and herbs. Cook over a low heat until the onions are very soft and the moisture has evaporated, about 45 minutes. Season with salt and pepper.

4 Preheat the oven to the highest setting. Oil a 13 × 9 in (33 × 23 cm) baking tray.

5 ▼ Transfer the risen dough onto a lightly floured surface. Punch down the dough and knead it briefly. Roll it out into a rectangle to fit the baking tray. Lay the dough on the tray and press it up the edges of the tray.

6 Brush the dough with 1 tablespoon olive oil. Discard the bay leaf, and spoon the onion mixture onto the dough. Spread it out evenly, leaving a ½ in (1 cm) border around the edge.

7 ▲ Arrange the anchovies and olives on top of the onions. Drizzle the remaining 2 tablespoons olive oil over the top.

8 Bake the pizza until the edges are puffed and browned, 15–20 minutes.

Spicy Sausage Pizza

SERVES 2–3

2 tbsp cornmeal

4 fl oz (125 ml) tomato sauce

8 oz (225 g) pepperoni sausage, cut in thin slices

8 oz (225 g) mozzarella cheese, grated

Pizza Dough (page 126, Broccoli and Goat Cheese Pizza)

1 Make the pizza dough as directed in steps 1–3 of Broccoli and Goat Cheese Pizza (page 126).

2 Preheat a 475°F/240°C/gas 9 oven. Oil a 12 in (30 cm) round pizza pan and sprinkle with the cornmeal.

3 Transfer the risen dough to a lightly floured surface. Punch down the dough to deflate it and knead it briefly.

4 ▼ Roll out the dough to a 12 in (30 cm) round. Lay the dough on the pizza pan and press it down evenly.

5 ▲ Spread the tomato sauce evenly on the pizza base, leaving a ½ in (1 cm) rim of dough uncovered around the edge. Arrange the sausage slices on top. Sprinkle with the cheese.

6 Bake until the cheese melts and the edge of the pizza base is puffed and browned, 10–15 minutes.

Folded Pizza with Peppers and Aubergine

SERVES 2

3–4 tbsp olive oil

½ small aubergine, cut in ½ in (1 cm) sticks

½ red pepper, seeded and sliced

½ yellow pepper, seeded and sliced

1 small onion, halved and sliced

1 garlic clove, crushed

salt and pepper

4 oz (125 g) mozzarella cheese, chopped

Pizza Dough (page 126, Broccoli and Goat Cheese Pizza)

1 Make the pizza dough as directed in steps 1–3 of Broccoli and Goat Cheese Pizza (page 126).

2 Heat 3 tbsp olive oil in a frying pan. Add the aubergine and cook until golden, about 6–8 minutes. Add the pepper strips, onion and garlic, with more oil if necessary. Cook, stirring occasionally, until softened, about 5 minutes longer. Season to taste.

3 Preheat a 475°F/240°C/gas 9 oven.

4 Transfer the risen pizza dough to a lightly floured surface. Punch down the dough to deflate it and knead it briefly. Divide the dough in half.

5 Roll out each piece of dough into a 7 in (18 cm) round. With the back of a knife, make an indentation across the centre of each round to mark it into halves.

6 ▲ Spoon half of the vegetable mixture onto one side of each dough round. Divide the cheese evenly between them.

7 ▲ Fold the dough over to enclose the filling. Pinch the edges to seal them securely.

8 Set the folded pizza on an oiled baking sheet. Bake until puffed and browned, 20–25 minutes. To serve, break or cut each pizza in half.

Spicy Sausage Pizza (top), Folded Pizza with Peppers and Aubergine

Pizza Toasts with Cheesy Topping

SERVES 4

2 small aubergines, cut across into thin slices (about 8 oz/225 g)
1 tbsp salt
4 fl oz (125 ml) olive oil
1 garlic clove, crushed with the side of a knife
8 slices French bread, ½ in (1 cm) thick
8 oz (225 g) Mozzarella cheese, cut into 8 slices
3 tbsp chopped fresh chives
3 tbsp chopped fresh basil

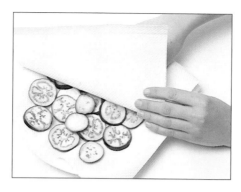

1 ▲ Put the aubergine slices in a colander and sprinkle with the salt. Let stand at least 30 minutes to drain. Rinse the aubergine slices under cold water, then blot dry with kitchen paper.

2 Heat half the olive oil in a frying pan. Add the aubergine slices and fry until golden brown, about 5 minutes on each side. Add more oil if necessary when the slices are turned over. Drain on kitchen paper.

3 Preheat a 325°F/170°C/Gas 3 oven.

4 ▲ In a small bowl, combine the remaining olive oil and the garlic. Brush both sides of the bread slices with the garlic oil. Place the slices on a baking tray. Bake until golden brown, about 10 minutes.

5 Preheat the grill.

6 ▲ Top each slice of garlic bread with a slice of aubergine and a slice of Mozzarella. Arrange on a baking tray.

7 Grill about 3 in (8 cm) from the heat until the cheese melts, 5–7 minutes. Sprinkle the toasts with the chopped herbs before serving.

Mini Tomato Pastry 'Pizzas'

SERVES 6

4 large or 8 small sheets of frozen filo pastry, thawed

2 fl oz (65 ml) olive oil

1 lb (450 g) tomatoes, peeled, seeded and diced

2 oz (55 g) Parmesan cheese, grated

4 oz (115 g) feta cheese, crumbled

9 black olives, stoned and halved

¼ tsp dried oregano

½ tsp fresh thyme leaves, or ⅛ tsp dried thyme

salt and pepper

fresh thyme or basil, for garnishing

1 Preheat a 350°F/180°C/Gas 4 oven. Grease 2 baking trays.

2 ▲ Stack the filo sheets. With a sharp knife, cut into 24 × 6 in (15 cm) rounds, using a small plate as a guide.

3 ▲ Lay 3 filo rounds on each baking tray. Brush the rounds lightly with olive oil. Lay another pastry round on top of each oiled round and brush it with oil. Continue layering the pastry rounds, oiling each one, to make 6 stacks of 4 rounds each.

4 Bake the filo bases until they are crisp and golden brown, about 5 minutes.

5 ▲ In a bowl, combine the tomatoes, cheeses, olives and herbs. Mix well. Season with salt and pepper.

6 ▲ Spoon the tomato mixture on top of the filo pastry bases, leaving the edges bare. Return to the oven to bake until heated through, about 5 minutes.

7 Serve hot, garnished with fresh herb sprigs.

Couscous with Vegetables

SERVES 4

2 tbsp olive oil

8 button onions, peeled

1 red pepper, seeded and quartered

1 leek, cut across into 1 in (2.5 cm) lengths

¼ tsp saffron strands

½ tsp turmeric

¼ tsp cayenne pepper

1 tsp ground ginger

1 × 3 in (8 cm) cinnamon stick

3 large carrots, cut diagonally into 1 in (2.5 cm) lengths

1 swede, peeled and cubed

2 potatoes, peeled and quartered

1 × 16 oz (450 g) can chopped tomatoes

1¼ pt (750 ml) chicken stock

salt and pepper

2 courgettes, cut across into 1 in (2.5 cm) lengths

4 oz (115 g) whole green beans, trimmed

1 × 15 oz (420 g) can chick peas, drained

2 tbsp chopped fresh coriander

2 tbsp chopped fresh parsley

FOR THE COUSCOUS

1 pt (575 ml) water

½ tsp salt

9 oz (250 g) instant couscous

1 Heat the oil in a large saucepan or cast iron casserole. Add the onions, red pepper and leek. Cook for 2–3 minutes.

~ **COOK'S TIP** ~

This couscous makes a filling vegetarian meal, and the recipe can be doubled or tripled. When multiplying a recipe, increase spices by less and taste.

2 ▲ Stir in the saffron, turmeric, cayenne, ginger and cinnamon stick.

3 ▲ Add the carrots, swede, potatoes, tomatoes and chicken stock. Season with salt. Bring to the boil. Reduce the heat to low, cover and simmer until the vegetables are nearly tender, about 25 minutes.

4 ▲ Meanwhile, for the couscous, put the water and salt in a saucepan and bring to the boil. Stir in the couscous. Remove the pan from the heat, cover and set aside until all the liquid is absorbed, about 10 minutes.

5 ▲ Stir the courgettes, green beans and chick peas into the vegetable mixture. Simmer 5 minutes longer.

6 ▲ Stir in the herbs and add pepper to taste.

7 ▲ Lightly fluff the couscous grains with a fork. Pile the couscous in a mound in the middle of a shallow, round platter. Spoon the vegetables over the couscous and serve.

Tangy Bulgur Wheat Salad

SERVES 6

4 oz (115 g) fine bulgur wheat

8 fl oz (250 ml) water

3 oz (85 g) fresh parsley, finely chopped

4 tbsp chopped fresh mint, or 2 tbsp dried mint

2 spring onions, finely chopped

½ small red onion, finely chopped

1 large tomato, chopped

2 fl oz (65 ml) olive oil

3 fl oz (85 ml) fresh lemon juice

salt and pepper

½ head of cos lettuce, leaves separated

1 Place the bulgur wheat in a bowl. Pour the water over the wheat. Let stand until the wheat swells and softens, about 30 minutes.

2 ▲ A handful at a time, squeeze excess water out of the bulgur wheat and put it in a mixing bowl.

3 ▲ Add the parsley, mint, spring onions, red onion and tomato to the bulgur wheat. Stir in the olive oil and lemon juice. Season to taste.

4 Line a large serving platter with the lettuce leaves. Pile the bulgur wheat salad in the middle.

Cheesy Vegetarian Slice

SERVES 6

1¼ pt (750 ml) water

¼ tsp salt

4 oz (115 g) instant polenta

1 egg

6 oz (175 g) Cheddar cheese, grated

1 oz (30 g) butter or margarine

⅛ tsp cayenne pepper

1 Preheat a 350°F/180°C/Gas 4 oven. Grease a 13 × 9 in (33 × 23 cm) baking dish.

2 Put the water and salt in a medium saucepan and bring to the boil.

~ **COOK'S TIP** ~

Served with salad or a tomato sauce, this makes a delicious snack. Try it instead of rice or potatoes with a main course, too.

3 ▲ Stir in the polenta. Reduce the heat to low, cover the pan and cook the polenta until thickened, 5–7 minutes, stirring occasionally.

4 ▲ In a small bowl, beat the egg lightly. Add a large spoonful of the cooked polenta and stir well to mix.

5 Stir the egg mixture into the remaining cooked polenta. Add two-thirds of the cheese, the butter, and the cayenne. Stir over low heat until the cheese melts.

6 ▲ Transfer the mixture to the prepared dish. Sprinkle the remaining cheese over the top. Bake until the cheesy polenta is set and golden on top, 35–40 minutes. Let cool 5 minutes before cutting and serving.

Tangy Bulgur Wheat Salad (top), Cheesy Vegetarian Slice

Mixed Rice Ring

SERVES 8

2 tbsp vegetable oil

1 large onion, chopped

12 oz (350 g) mixed long-grain and wild rice

2 pt (1.25 litres) chicken stock

2½ oz (75 g) currants

salt

6 spring onions, cut diagonally into ¼ in (5 mm) lengths

parsley sprigs, for garnishing

1 Oil a 2¾ pt (1.75 litre) ring.

2 ▼ Heat the oil in a large saucepan. Add the onion and cook until softened, about 5 minutes.

3 ▲ Add the rice to the pan and stir well to coat the rice with the oil.

4 ▲ Stir in the chicken stock and bring to the boil.

5 Reduce the heat to low. Stir the currants into the rice mixture. Add salt to taste. Cover and simmer until the rice is tender and the stock has been absorbed, about 20 minutes.

6 Drain the rice if necessary and transfer it to a mixing bowl. Stir in the spring onions.

7 ▲ Pack the rice mixture into the prepared mould. Unmould it onto a warmed serving platter. If you like, put parsley sprigs into the centre of the ring before serving.

Green and Orange Riso

SERVES 4

2 pt (1.25 litres) chicken stock

1½ oz (45 g) butter or margarine

1 small onion, chopped

2 oz (55 g) peeled and coarsely grated acorn squash or pumpkin

9 oz (250 g) short-grain rice

1 courgette, quartered lengthwise and chopped

5 oz (140 g) frozen peas, thawed

1½ oz (45 g) Parmesan cheese, grated

salt and pepper

1 In a saucepan, bring the stock to a simmer. Keep it simmering gently.

2 Melt one-third of the butter or margarine in a heavy saucepan. Add the onion and cook until softened, about 5 minutes.

3 ▲ Add the grated squash to the onion. Cook 1 minute, stirring.

4 ▲ Add the rice and stir to coat all the grains well with butter. Cook 1 minute, stirring.

5 Add a ladleful of the simmering stock to the rice. Cook, stirring frequently, until the stock is absorbed. Continue adding the stock, one ladleful at a time, allowing each addition to be absorbed before adding the next, and stirring frequently.

6 ▲ After about 5 minutes, stir in the courgette pieces. After about 10 minutes, stir in the peas. The risotto will be cooked in about 20 minutes.

7 ▲ Remove the pan from the heat. Add the remaining butter or margarine and the Parmesan and stir well. Season with salt and pepper. If you like, serve in hollowed-out cooked acorn squash halves.

Red Beans and Rice

SERVES 4

1 onion, chopped

1 green pepper, seeded and chopped

4 rashers of bacon, chopped

1 garlic clove, chopped

6 oz (170 g) long-grain rice

2–3 tsp chilli powder

2 tsp fresh thyme leaves or ½ tsp dried thyme

16 fl oz (450 ml) canned chopped tomatoes

8 fl oz (250 ml) chicken or beef stock

salt and pepper

1 × 15 oz (420 g) can red kidney beans, drained and rinsed

1 ▼ In a medium saucepan, cook the onion, green pepper, bacon and garlic until the vegetables are softened and the bacon has rendered its fat, about 5 minutes.

2 ▲ Add the rice and stir until all the grains are coated with bacon fat. Stir in the chilli powder and cook 1 minute.

3 ▲ Add the thyme, chopped tomatoes and stock and stir well. Season with salt and pepper. Bring to the boil.

4 Reduce the heat to low, cover the pan and simmer until the rice is nearly tender, about 15 minutes.

5 ▲ Stir in the kidney beans. Cover again and simmer until the rice is tender and all the stock has been absorbed, about 5 minutes longer.

6 Fluff the rice and beans with a fork, then transfer to a warmed serving dish.

Nut Pilaf

SERVES 4

1 oz (30 g) butter or margarine

1 onion, finely chopped

12 oz (350 g) long-grain brown rice

½ tsp finely grated lemon rind

16 fl oz (450 ml) chicken stock

16 fl oz (450 ml) water

¼ tsp salt

4 spring onions, finely chopped

2 tbsp fresh lemon juice

1½ oz (45 g) pecan halves, toasted

1 ▲ Melt the butter or margarine in a medium saucepan. Add the onion and cook until softened, about 5 minutes.

2 ▲ Stir in the rice and cook 1 minute, stirring.

3 ▲ Add the lemon rind, chicken stock, water and salt and stir well. Bring to the boil. Reduce the heat to low, cover the pan and simmer until the rice is tender and all the liquid is absorbed, 30–35 minutes.

4 ▼ Remove the pan from the heat and let stand 5 minutes, still covered. Stir in the spring onions, lemon juice and pecan halves. Transfer to a warmed serving dish.

Fried Rice with Prawns and Asparagus

SERVES 4

3 tbsp vegetable oil

12 oz (350 g) asparagus, cut diagonally into 1 in (2.5 cm) lengths

3 oz (85 g) brown or button mushrooms, sliced

12 oz (350 g) cooked long-grain rice

1 tsp finely grated fresh root ginger

8 oz (225 g) cooked peeled prawns, deveined

4 oz (115 g) canned water chestnuts, drained and sliced

3 tbsp soy sauce

pepper

~ VARIATION ~

Ingredients for fried rice are infinitely variable. Instead of prawns, try scallops or cubes of firm-fleshed fish.

1 ▲ Heat the oil in a wok over high heat. Add the asparagus and mushrooms and stir-fry, 3–4 minutes.

2 ▲ Stir in the rice and ginger. Cook, stirring, until heated through, about 3 minutes.

3 ▲ Add the prawns and stir-fry for 1 minute.

4 ▲ Add the water chestnuts and soy sauce and stir-fry 1 minute longer. Season with pepper and serve.

Saffron Rice

SERVES 6

4 tbsp butter or margarine

⅛ tsp crumbled saffron strands

1 lb (450 g) long-grain rice

1¾ pt (1 litre) chicken stock

½ tsp salt

~ COOK'S TIP ~

If preferred, bring the saffron rice to the boil in a flameproof casserole, then transfer to a preheated 375°F/190°C/Gas 5 oven.

1 Melt the butter or margarine in a large saucepan. Stir in the saffron.

2 ▲ Add the rice and stir to coat all the grains well with the saffron butter.

3 ▼ Stir in the stock and salt. Bring to the boil. Reduce the heat to low, cover and simmer until the rice is tender and all the stock has been absorbed, about 20 minutes.

4 Fluff the rice grains with a fork before serving.

Fried Rice with Prawns and Asparagus (top), Saffron Rice

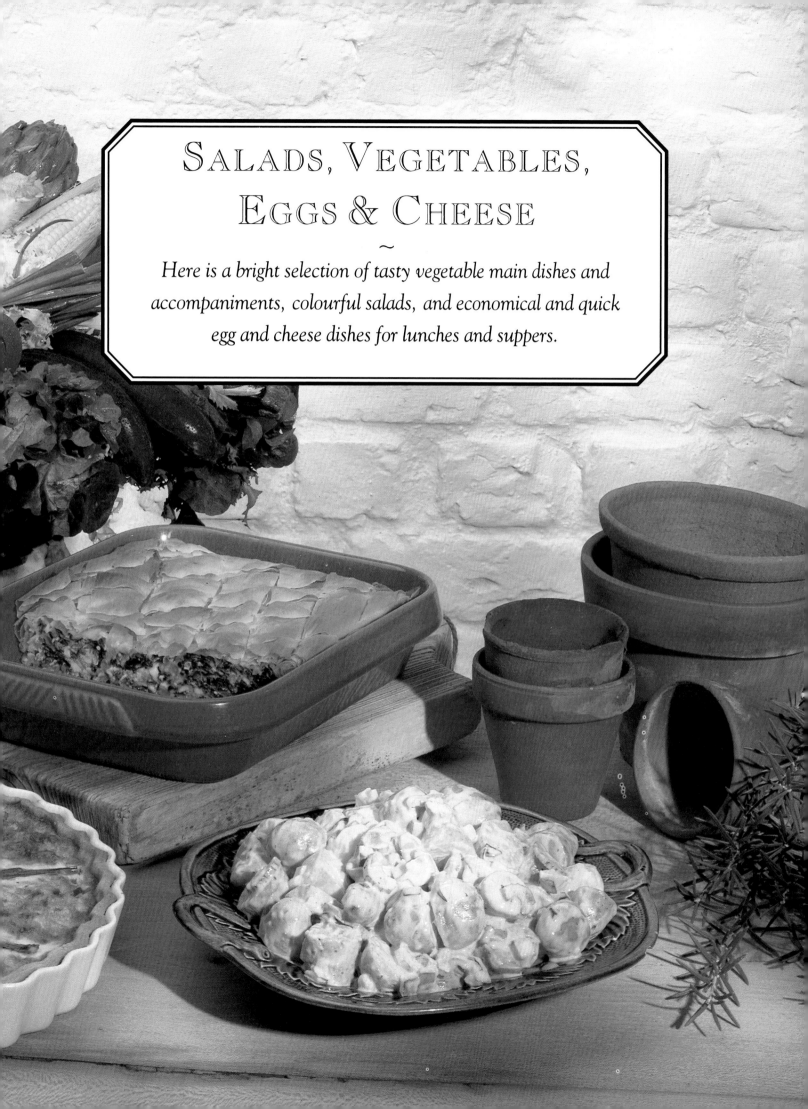

SALADS, VEGETABLES, EGGS & CHEESE

~

Here is a bright selection of tasty vegetable main dishes and accompaniments, colourful salads, and economical and quick egg and cheese dishes for lunches and suppers.

Avocado, Grapefruit and Melon Salad

SERVES 6

1 pink grapefruit

1 yellow grapefruit

1 cantaloup melon

2 large, ripe but firm avocados

2 tbsp fresh lemon juice

2 tbsp vegetable oil

1 tbsp clear honey

3 tbsp chopped fresh mint

salt and pepper

fresh mint leaves, for garnishing

1 ▲ Peel the grapefruit. Cut out the segments, leaving the membranes. Put the segments in a bowl.

2 Cut the melon in half. Remove the seeds and discard them. With a melon baller, scoop out balls from the melon flesh. Add the melon balls to the grapefruit sections. Chill the fruit at least 30 minutes.

3 ▲ Cut the avocados in half and discard the stones. Cut each half in two. Peel off the skin, then cut the flesh into small pieces.

4 ▲ Toss the avocado pieces in the lemon juice. Using a slotted spoon, transfer the avocado to the grapefruit mixture.

5 ▲ For the dressing, whisk the oil into the reserved lemon juice. Stir in the honey, chopped mint and salt and pepper to taste.

6 Pour the dressing over the fruit mixture and toss gently. Garnish with mint leaves and serve immediately.

Sweet and Savoury Salad

SERVES 4

1 medium red onion, thinly sliced into rings

salt and pepper

2 oranges, peeled and cut in segments

1 firm jícama, peeled and cut in matchstick strips, or drained canned water chestnuts

2 heads of radicchio, cored, or 1 head of red leaf lettuce, leaves separated

3 tbsp chopped fresh parsley

3 tbsp chopped fresh basil

1 tbsp white wine vinegar

2 fl oz (65 ml) walnut oil

1 ▲ Put the onion in a colander and sprinkle with 1 teaspoon salt. Let drain 15 minutes.

2 In a mixing bowl combine the orange and jícama or water chestnuts.

3 Spread out the radicchio or lettuce leaves in a large shallow bowl or serving platter.

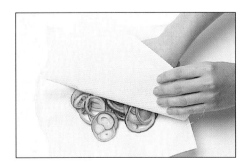

4 ▲ Rinse the onion and dry on kitchen paper. Toss it with the jícama or water chestnuts and orange.

5 ▼ Arrange the jícama or water chestnut, orange and onion mixture on top of the radicchio leaves. Sprinkle with the parsley and basil.

6 ▲ Combine the vinegar, oil and salt and pepper to taste in a screwtop jar. Shake well to combine. Pour the dressing over the salad and serve immediately.

Crispy Coleslaw

SERVES 6

12 oz (350 g) green or white cabbage, cut in wedges and cored

4 oz (115 g) red cabbage, cored

3 spring onions, finely chopped

2 medium carrots, grated

1 tsp sugar

2 tbsp fresh lemon juice

2 tsp distilled white vinegar

4 fl oz (125 ml) soured cream

4 fl oz (125 ml) mayonnaise

¾ tsp celery seeds

salt and pepper

1 ▼ Slice the green and red cabbage thinly across the leaves.

2 Place the cabbage in a mixing bowl and add the spring onions and carrots. Toss to combine.

3 In a small bowl, combine the sugar, lemon juice, vinegar, soured cream, mayonnaise and celery seeds.

4 ▲ Pour the mayonnaise dressing over the vegetables. Season with salt and pepper. Stir until well coated. Spoon into a serving bowl.

Tangy Potato Salad

SERVES 8

3 lb (1.35 kg) small new potatoes

2 tbsp white wine vinegar

1 tbsp Dijon mustard

3 tbsp vegetable or olive oil

3 oz (85 g) chopped red onion

salt and pepper

4 fl oz (125 ml) mayonnaise

2 tbsp chopped fresh tarragon, or 1½ tsp dried tarragon

1 celery stick, thinly sliced

1 Cook the unpeeled potatoes in boiling salted water until tender, 15–20 minutes. Drain.

2 In a small bowl, mix together the vinegar and mustard until the mustard dissolves. Whisk in the oil.

3 ▲ When the potatoes are cool enough to handle, slice them into a large mixing bowl.

4 ▲ Add the onion to the potatoes and pour the dressing over them. Season, then toss gently to combine. Let stand at least 30 minutes.

5 ▲ Mix together the mayonnaise and tarragon. Gently stir into the potatoes, along with the celery. Taste and adjust the seasoning before serving.

~ **VARIATION** ~

Substitute 3 tablespoons dry white wine for the wine vinegar, if preferred. When available, use small red potatoes to give a nice colour to the salad.

Crispy Coleslaw (top), Tangy Potato Salad

Caesar Salad

SERVES 4

2 eggs

1 garlic clove, crushed

½ tsp salt

4 fl oz (125 ml) olive oil

juice of 1 lemon

¼ tsp Worcestershire sauce

1 lb (450 g) cos lettuce, torn into bite-
  sized pieces

1½ oz (45 g) Parmesan cheese, freshly
  grated

pepper

8 canned anchovy fillets, drained and
  blotted dry on kitchen paper
  (optional)

FOR THE CROUTONS

1 garlic clove

¼ tsp salt

2 fl oz (65 ml) olive oil

4–6 slices French bread, cubed

1 Preheat a 350°F/180°C/Gas 4 oven.

2 ▲ For the croûtons, crush the garlic with the salt in a mixing bowl and mix in the oil. Add the bread cubes to the bowl and toss to coat with the garlic oil.

3 Spread the bread cubes on a baking tray. Bake until golden brown, 20–25 minutes.

4 Meanwhile, put the eggs in a small pan of boiling water and simmer gently for 7 minutes. Transfer the eggs to a bowl of cold water and shell them as soon as they are cool enough to handle.

5 ▼ Mash the garlic clove with the salt in the bottom of a salad bowl. Whisk in the olive oil, lemon juice and Worcestershire sauce.

6 Add the lettuce to the salad bowl and toss well to coat with the dressing.

7 Add the Parmesan cheese and season with pepper. Add the croûtons and toss well to combine.

8 Cut the hard-boiled eggs in quarters. Arrange on top of the salad with the anchovies, if using. Serve immediately.

Green Salad with Blue Cheese Dressing

SERVES 6

4 handfuls mixed salad leaves, torn in
  bite-size pieces

1 small bunch of lamb's lettuce
  (mâche), rocket or watercress

FOR THE DRESSING

4 fl oz (125 ml) plain yoghurt

1½ tsp white wine vinegar

½ tsp sugar

1 tbsp fresh lemon juice

1 garlic clove, crushed

1 oz (30 g) blue cheese, crumbled

1 ▼ For the dressing, combine the yoghurt, wine vinegar, sugar, lemon juice and garlic in a small bowl and mix well. Fold in the cheese. The dressing should be lumpy.

2 ▲ Put the salad leaves in a salad bowl. Add the dressing and toss until all the leaves are coated. Serve immediately.

Caesar Salad (top), Green Salad with Blue Cheese Dressing

Spinach and Bacon Salad

SERVES 4

1 hard-boiled egg
3 fl oz (85 ml) white wine vinegar
1 tsp Dijon mustard
2 tbsp vegetable or olive oil
salt and pepper
1 lb (450 g) fresh young spinach leaves
2 oz (55 g) small mushrooms, sliced
3 rashers of bacon
1 medium onion, chopped
2 garlic cloves, crushed

1 Separate the egg yolk and white. Chop the egg white and set aside.

2 ▲ To make the dressing, press the egg yolk through a sieve into a bowl. Whisk in the vinegar, mustard, oil and salt and pepper to taste.

3 Put the spinach in a salad bowl with the mushrooms.

4 In a small frying pan, fry the bacon until crisp. Remove the bacon and drain on kitchen paper.

5 ▼ When cool, crumble the bacon over the spinach.

6 Add the onion and garlic to the bacon fat in the frying pan and cook until softened, about 5 minutes, stirring frequently.

7 Pour the onion and garlic over the spinach, with the bacon fat. Add the dressing and toss well to combine. Sprinkle the egg white on top and serve immediately.

Warm Red Cabbage Salad with Spicy Sausage

SERVES 4

1 lb (450 g) red cabbage, cut in wedges and cored
2 fl oz (65 ml) olive oil
2 shallots or 1 small onion, chopped
2 garlic cloves, chopped
3 tbsp cider vinegar
4 oz (115 g) chorizo or other cooked spicy sausage, cut diagonally in ¼ in (5 mm) slices
salt and pepper
2 tbsp chopped fresh chives
2 tbsp chopped fresh parsley

1 Slice the cabbage wedges very thinly across the leaves.

2 ▲ Heat the oil in a frying pan. Add the shallots and garlic and cook until softened, about 4 minutes. Transfer from the pan to a salad bowl using a slotted spoon.

3 Add the cabbage to the hot oil and cook until wilted, about 10 minutes, stirring occasionally. Add 1 tablespoon of the vinegar and cook 1 minute longer, stirring. Transfer the cabbage and the oil from the pan to the salad bowl.

4 ▼ Add the sausage slices to the pan and fry until well browned. Transfer the sausage to the salad bowl using the slotted spoon.

5 Pour the remaining vinegar over the salad and toss well to combine. Season with salt and pepper. Sprinkle with the chopped herbs and serve.

Spinach and Bacon Salad (top), Warm Red Cabbage Salad with Spicy Sausage

Pasta, Olive and Avocado Salad

SERVES 6

8 oz (225 g) pasta spirals, or other small pasta shapes

4 oz (115 g) drained canned sweetcorn, or frozen sweetcorn, thawed

½ red pepper, seeded and diced

8 black olives, stoned and sliced

3 spring onions, finely chopped

2 medium avocados

FOR THE DRESSING

2 sun-dried tomato halves, loose-packed (not preserved in oil)

1½ tbsp balsamic or white wine vinegar

1½ tbsp red wine vinegar

½ garlic clove, crushed

½ tsp salt

5 tbsp olive oil

1 tbsp chopped fresh basil

1 ▼ For the dressing, drop the sun-dried tomatoes into a pan containing 1 in (2.5 cm) of boiling water and simmer until tender, about 3 minutes. Drain and chop finely.

2 ▲ Combine the tomatoes, vinegars, garlic and salt in a food processor. With the machine on, add the oil in a stream. Stir in the basil.

3 Cook the pasta in a large pan of boiling salted water until just tender (check packet instructions for timing). Drain well.

4 ▲ In a large bowl, combine the pasta, sweetcorn, red pepper, olives and spring onions. Add the dressing and toss well together.

5 ▲ Just before serving, peel the avocados and cut the flesh into cubes. Mix gently into the pasta salad and serve at room temperature.

Ham and Bean Salad

SERVES 8

6 oz (175 g) dried black-eyed beans

1 onion

1 carrot

8 oz (225 g) smoked ham, diced

3 medium tomatoes, peeled, seeded and diced

salt and pepper

FOR THE DRESSING

2 garlic cloves, crushed

3 tbsp olive oil

3 tbsp red wine vinegar

2 tbsp vegetable oil

1 tbsp fresh lemon juice

1 tbsp chopped fresh basil, or 1 tsp dried basil

1 tbsp whole-grain mustard

1 tsp soy sauce

½ tsp dried oregano

½ tsp caster sugar

¼ tsp Worcestershire sauce

½ tsp chilli sauce

1 Soak the black-eyed beans in water to cover overnight. Drain.

2 ▲ Put the beans in a large saucepan and add the onion and carrot. Cover with fresh cold water and bring to the boil. Lower the heat and simmer until the beans are tender, about 1 hour. Drain, reserving the onion and carrot. Transfer the beans to a salad bowl.

3 ▼ Finely chop the onion and carrot. Toss with the beans. Stir in the ham and tomatoes.

4 For the dressing, combine all the ingredients in a small bowl and whisk to mix.

5 ▲ Pour the dressing over the beans. Season with salt and pepper. Toss to combine.

Egg, Bacon and Avocado Salad

SERVES 4

1 large head of cos lettuce, sliced into strips across the leaves

8 rashers of bacon, fried until crisp and crumbled

2 large avocados, peeled and diced

6 hard-boiled eggs, chopped

2 beef tomatoes, peeled, seeded and chopped

6 oz (170 g) blue cheese, crumbled

FOR THE DRESSING

1 garlic clove, crushed

1 tsp sugar

½ tbsp fresh lemon juice

1½ tbsp red wine vinegar

4 fl oz (125 ml) groundnut oil

salt and pepper

1 For the dressing, combine all the ingredients in a screwtop jar and shake well.

2 ▲ On a large rectangular or oval platter, spread out the lettuce to make a bed.

3 ▲ Reserve the bacon, and arrange the remaining ingredients in rows, beginning with the avocados. Sprinkle the bacon on top.

4 Pour the dressing over the salad just before serving.

Spicy Sweetcorn Salad

SERVES 4

2 tbsp vegetable oil

1 lb (450 g) drained canned sweetcorn, or frozen sweetcorn, thawed

1 green pepper, seeded and diced

1 small fresh red chilli pepper, seeded and finely diced

4 spring onions, cut diagonally into ½ in (1 cm) lengths

3 tbsp chopped fresh parsley

8 oz (225 g) cherry tomatoes, halved

salt and pepper

FOR THE DRESSING

½ tsp sugar

2 tbsp white wine vinegar

½ tsp Dijon mustard

1 tbsp chopped fresh basil, or 1 tsp dried basil

1 tbsp mayonnaise

¼ tsp chilli sauce

1 Heat the oil in a frying pan. Add the sweetcorn, pepper, chilli pepper and spring onions. Cook over a medium heat until softened, about 5 minutes, stirring frequently.

2 ▲ Transfer the vegetables to a salad bowl. Stir in the parsley and tomatoes.

3 ▲ For the dressing, combine all the ingredients in a small bowl and whisk together. Pour the dressing over the sweetcorn mixture. Season with salt and pepper. Toss well to combine, and serve.

Egg, Bacon and Avocado Salad (top), Spicy Sweetcorn Salad

Scalloped Potatoes

SERVES 6

2½ lb (1.2 kg) potatoes, peeled and cut in ⅛ in (3 mm) slices

salt and pepper

1 large onion, thinly sliced

1 oz (30 g) plain flour

2 oz (55 g) butter or margarine, cut in small pieces

6 oz (175 g) Cheddar cheese, grated

7 fl oz (200 ml) milk

16 fl oz (500 ml) single cream

1 Preheat a 350°F/180°C/Gas 4 oven. Butter a 10 in (25 cm) oval gratin dish.

2 Layer one-quarter of the potato slices in the prepared dish. Season with salt and pepper.

3 ▼ Layer one-quarter of the sliced onion over the potatoes. Sprinkle with one-quarter of the flour and dot with one-quarter of the butter or margarine. Sprinkle with one-quarter of the cheese.

4 Continue layering these ingredients, making 4 layers.

5 ▲ Heat the milk and single cream in a small saucepan. Pour the mixture evenly over the potatoes.

6 Cover the gratin dish with foil. Place it in the oven and bake for 1 hour. Remove the foil and bake until the potatoes are tender and the top is golden, 15–20 minutes longer.

New Potatoes with Savoury Butter

SERVES 6

1¼ lb (575 g) small new potatoes

2 oz (55 g) butter or margarine

3 shallots or 1 small to medium onion, finely chopped

2 garlic cloves, crushed

salt and pepper

1 tsp chopped fresh tarragon

1 tsp chopped fresh chives

1 tsp chopped fresh parsley

1 Bring a saucepan of salted water to the boil. Add the potatoes and cook until just tender, 15–20 minutes. Drain well.

2 ▼ Melt the butter or margarine in a frying pan. Add the shallots or onion and garlic and cook over low heat until softened, about 5 minutes.

3 ▲ Add the potatoes to the pan and stir well to mix with the savoury butter. Season with salt and pepper. Cook, stirring, until the potatoes are heated through.

4 Transfer the potatoes to a warmed serving bowl. Sprinkle with the chopped herbs before serving.

Scalloped Potatoes (top), New Potatoes with Savoury Butter

Mashed Potatoes with Garlic

SERVES 6

2–3 heads of garlic, according to taste, cloves separated

2 oz (55 g) butter or margarine

2½ lb (1.2 kg) potatoes, peeled and quartered

salt and pepper

4 fl oz (125 ml) whipping cream

3 tbsp chopped fresh chives

1 Drop the garlic cloves into a pan of boiling water and boil 2 minutes. Drain and peel.

2 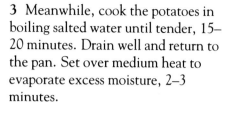 Melt half the butter or margarine in a small saucepan over a low heat. Add the peeled garlic. Cover and cook until very soft, 20–25 minutes, stirring frequently.

3 Meanwhile, cook the potatoes in boiling salted water until tender, 15–20 minutes. Drain well and return to the pan. Set over medium heat to evaporate excess moisture, 2–3 minutes.

4  Push the potatoes through a potato ricer or mash them with a potato masher. Return them to the saucepan and beat in the remaining butter or margarine, in two batches. Season with salt and pepper.

5 ▲ Remove the pan of garlic from the heat and mash the garlic and butter together with a fork until smooth. Stir in the cream. Return to the heat and bring just to the boil.

6 Beat the garlic cream into the potatoes, 1 tablespoon at a time. Reheat the potatoes if necessary.

7 Fold most of the chives into the potatoes. Transfer the potatoes to a warmed serving bowl and sprinkle the remaining chives on top.

Candied Sweet Potatoes

SERVES 8

3 lb (1.35 kg) sweet potatoes, peeled

1½ oz (45 g) butter or margarine

4 fl oz (125 ml) maple syrup

¾ tsp ground ginger

1 tbsp fresh lemon juice

1 Preheat a 375°F/190°C/Gas 5 oven. Grease a large shallow baking dish.

2 ▲ Cut the potatoes in ½ in (1 cm) slices. Cook them in boiling water for 10 minutes. Drain. Let cool.

3 ▲ Melt the butter or margarine in a small saucepan over a medium heat. Stir in the maple syrup until well combined. Stir in the ginger. Simmer 1 minute, then add the lemon juice.

4 ▼ Arrange the potato slices in one layer in the prepared baking dish, overlapping them slightly.

5 ▲ Drizzle the maple syrup mixture evenly over the potatoes. Bake until the potatoes are tender and glazed, 30–35 minutes, spooning the cooking liquid over them once or twice.

Creamy Sweetcorn with Peppers

Serves 4

1 oz (30 g) butter or margarine

1 small red pepper, seeded and finely diced

1 small green pepper, seeded and finely diced

4 corn cobs, trimmed

4 fl oz (125 ml) whipping cream

salt and pepper

1 ▲ Melt the butter or margarine in a saucepan. Add the peppers and cook 5 minutes, stirring occasionally.

2 ▼ Cut the kernels off the corn cobs. Scrape the cobs with the back of a knife to extract the milky liquid. Alternatively, use a corn scraper to remove the kernels and liquid.

~ **VARIATION** ~

1 lb (450 g) frozen sweetcorn, thawed, can be substituted if fresh corn cobs are not available.

3 ▲ Add the sweetcorn with the liquid to the saucepan. Stir in the cream. Bring to the boil and simmer until thickened and the sweetcorn is tender, 3–4 minutes. Season with salt and pepper.

Fried Okra

Serves 6

1½ lb (700 g) okra

2 oz (55 g) cornmeal, or polenta

⅛ tsp black pepper

3 fl oz (85 ml) bacon dripping or oil

¾ tsp salt

~ **COOK'S TIP** ~

When removing the stems of the okra, slice through the point where it joins the vegetable. Cutting into the vegetable allows the release of the viscous insides.

1 Wash the okra well and drain in a colander. Cut off the stems.

2 ▲ Combine the cornmeal and pepper in a mixing bowl. Add the still damp okra and toss to coat evenly with cornmeal.

3 ▼ Heat the bacon drippings or oil in a frying pan. Add the okra and fry until tender and golden, 4–5 minutes. Drain on kitchen paper.

4 Sprinkle the fried okra with the salt just before serving.

Creamy Sweetcorn with Peppers (top), Fried Okra

Brussels Sprouts with Chestnuts

SERVES 6

1 lb (450 g) Brussels sprouts, trimmed

4 oz (115 g) butter or margarine

3 celery sticks, cut diagonally in ½ in (1 cm) lengths

1 large onion, thinly sliced

1 × 14 oz (400 g) can whole chestnuts in brine, drained and rinsed

¼ tsp grated nutmeg

salt and pepper

grated rind of 1 lemon

2 ▲ Melt the butter or margarine in a frying pan over low heat. Add the celery and onion and cook until softened, about 5 minutes.

1 ▲ Drop the Brussels sprouts into a pan of boiling salted water and cook 3–4 minutes. Drain well.

3 ▲ Raise the heat to medium and add the chestnuts and Brussels sprouts to the frying pan.

4 Stir in the nutmeg and salt and pepper to taste. Cook until piping hot, about 2 minutes, stirring frequently.

5 ▲ Stir in the grated lemon rind. Transfer to a warmed serving dish.

~ **VARIATION** ~

For a tasty alternative, substitute grated orange rind for the lemon rind, especially when serving with pork or turkey.

Green Peas and Baby Onions

SERVES 6

½ oz (15 g) butter or margarine

12 baby onions, peeled

1 small butterhead lettuce, shredded

10 oz (300 g) shelled fresh green peas or frozen peas, thawed

1 tsp sugar

2 tbsp water

salt and pepper

2 sprigs fresh mint

1 Melt the butter or margarine in a frying pan. Add the onions and cook over medium heat until they just begin to colour, about 10 minutes.

2 ▼ Add the lettuce, peas, sugar and water. Season with salt and pepper. Bring to a boil. Reduce the heat to low, cover and simmer until the peas are tender, about 15 minutes for fresh peas and 10 minutes for frozen peas, stirring occasionally.

3 ▲ Strip the mint leaves from the stems. Chop finely with a sharp knife. Stir the mint into the peas. Transfer to a warmed serving dish.

Brussels Sprouts with Chestnuts (top), Green Peas and Baby Onions

Broccoli and Cauliflower Bake

SERVES 6

| 1–1½ lb (450–700 g) broccoli, trimmed |
| 1–1½ lb (450–700 g) cauliflower, trimmed |

FOR THE CHEESE SAUCE

| 3 tbsp butter or margarine |
| 1 oz (30 g) plain flour |
| 12 fl oz (375 ml) milk |
| 3 oz (85 g) Cheddar cheese, grated |
| ⅛ tsp grated nutmeg |
| salt and pepper |

1 Preheat a 300°F/150°C/Gas 2 oven. Butter a 1¾ pt (1 litre) ovenproof bowl or round mould.

2 Break the broccoli into florets. Drop into a pan of boiling salted water and cook 5 minutes. Drain and rinse with cold water to stop the cooking. Drain thoroughly, then spread on kitchen paper to dry.

3 Break the cauliflower into florets. Drop into a pan of boiling salted water and cook 5 minutes. Drain and rinse with cold water. Drain thoroughly, then spread the florets on kitchen paper to dry.

4 ▲ Place a cluster of cauliflower on the bottom of the prepared bowl, stems pointing inwards. Add a layer of broccoli, heads against the side and stems pointing inwards. Fill the centre with smaller florets.

5 ▲ Add another layer of cauliflower florets. Finish with a layer of broccoli.

6 Cover the bowl with buttered foil. Bake until the vegetables are heated through, 10–15 minutes.

7 Meanwhile, for the sauce, melt the butter or margarine in a saucepan. Add the flour and cook 2 minutes, stirring. Stir in the milk. Bring to the boil, stirring constantly, and simmer until thickened, about 5 minutes. Stir in the cheese. Season with the nutmeg and salt and pepper to taste. Keep the sauce warm over a very low heat.

8 ▲ Hold a warmed serving plate over the top of the bowl, turn them over together and lift off the bowl. Serve the moulded vegetables with the cheese sauce.

Green Bean and Red Pepper Stir-Fry

SERVES 4

| 1 lb (450 g) fine green beans, cut diagonally in 1 in (2.5 cm) lengths |
| 2 tbsp olive oil |
| 1 red pepper, seeded and cut in matchstick strips |
| ½ tsp soy sauce |
| 1 tsp fresh lemon juice |

1 Drop the green beans into a pan of boiling salted water and cook 3 minutes. Drain and refresh in cold water. Pat dry with kitchen paper.

2 ▼ Heat the oil in a frying pan. Add the green beans and red pepper and stir-fry until just tender, about 2 minutes.

3 ▲ Remove the pan from the heat and stir in the soy sauce and lemon juice. Transfer the vegetables to a warmed serving dish.

Broccoli and Cauliflower Bake (top), Green Bean and Red Pepper Stir-Fry

Baked Onions with Sun-Dried Tomatoes

SERVES 4

1 lb (450 g) button onions
2 tsp chopped fresh rosemary, or ¾ tsp dried rosemary
2 garlic cloves, chopped
1 tbsp chopped fresh parsley
salt and pepper
4 fl oz (125 ml) sun-dried tomatoes in oil, drained and chopped
6 tbsp olive oil
1 tbsp white wine vinegar

1 Preheat a 300°F/150°C/Gas 2 oven. Grease a shallow baking dish.

2 ▼ Drop the onions into a pan of boiling water and cook 5 minutes. Drain in a colander.

3 ▲ Spread the onions in the bottom of the prepared baking dish.

4 ▲ Combine the rosemary, garlic, parsley, salt and pepper and sprinkle over the onions.

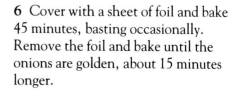

5 ▲ Scatter the tomatoes over the onions. Drizzle the olive oil and vinegar on top.

6 Cover with a sheet of foil and bake 45 minutes, basting occasionally. Remove the foil and bake until the onions are golden, about 15 minutes longer.

Special Stewed Tomatoes

SERVES 6

2 lb (900 g) very ripe tomatoes, stems
  removed

1 oz (30 g) butter or margarine

2 celery sticks, diced

1 small green pepper, seeded and
  diced

2 spring onions, finely chopped

salt and pepper

2 tbsp chopped fresh basil

1 Fill a mixing bowl with boiling
water and another bowl with iced
water. Three or four at a time, drop
the tomatoes into the boiling water
and leave them 30 seconds.

2 ▲ Remove the tomatoes with a
slotted spoon and transfer to the iced
water. When they are cool enough to
handle, remove the tomatoes from the
iced water.

3 ▲ Peel the tomatoes and cut them
into wedges.

4 ▼ Heat the butter or margarine in
a flameproof casserole or saucepan.
Add the celery, green pepper and
spring onions and cook until softened,
about 5 minutes.

~ **VARIATION** ~

To make stewed tomatoes into a
tomato sauce, cook uncovered in
a frying pan, stirring occasionally,
until thickened to the desired
consistency.

5 ▲ Stir in the tomatoes. Cover and
cook until the tomatoes are soft but
not mushy, 10–15 minutes, stirring
occasionally. Season with salt and
pepper.

6 Remove the pan from the heat and
stir in the basil.

Braised Red Cabbage with Apple

SERVES 6

2 lb (900 g) red cabbage, quartered and cored

salt and pepper

2 medium red onions, halved and thinly sliced

2 Red Delicious apples, peeled, cored, halved and thinly sliced

1½ tsp caraway seeds

3 tbsp light brown sugar

3 tbsp red wine vinegar

1 oz (30 g) butter or margarine, diced

1 Preheat a 400°F/200°C/Gas 6 oven.

2 Slice the cabbage quarters thinly across the leaves.

~ **VARIATION** ~

For a sharper flavour, substitute Granny Smith or other tart varieties of eating apple for the Red Delicious apples in this recipe.

3 ▲ Make a layer of one-quarter of the cabbage in a large, deep baking dish. Season with salt and pepper.

4 ▲ Layer one-third of the sliced onions and apples on top of the cabbage. Sprinkle with some of the caraway seeds and 1 tablespoon of the brown sugar.

5 Continue layering until all the ingredients have been used, ending with a layer of cabbage on top.

6 ▲ Pour in the vinegar and dot the top with the butter or margarine. Cover and bake 1 hour.

7 Remove the cover and continue baking until the cabbage is very tender and all the liquid has evaporated, about 30 minutes longer.

Glazed Carrots with Spring Onion

SERVES 6

1 lb (450 g) baby carrots, trimmed and peeled if necessary

1½ oz (45 g) butter or margarine

2 tbsp honey

2 tbsp fresh orange juice

8 oz (225 g) spring onions, cut diagonally into 1 in (2.5 cm) lengths

salt and pepper

1 Cook the carrots in boiling salted water or steam them until just tender, about 1? minutes. Drain if necessary.

2 ▼ In a frying pan, melt the butter or margarine with the honey and orange juice, stirring until the mixture is smooth and well combined.

3 ▲ Add the carrots and spring onions to the pan. Cook over medium heat, stirring occasionally, until the vegetables are heated through and glazed, about 5 minutes. Season with salt and pepper before serving.

Braised Red Cabbage with Apple (top), Glazed Carrots with Spring Onion

Spanish Omelette

SERVES 4

4 rashers of bacon

3 tbsp olive oil

1 onion, thinly sliced

½ small red pepper, seeded and sliced

½ small green pepper, seeded and sliced

1 large garlic clove, crushed

12 oz (350 g) small potatoes, cooked and sliced

4 eggs

2 tbsp single cream

salt and pepper

1 Preheat a 350°F/180°C/Gas 4 oven.

2 In a heavy 8 in (20 cm) frying pan with an ovenproof handle, fry the bacon until crisp. Drain on kitchen paper.

3 Pour off the bacon fat from the frying pan. Add 1 tablespoon oil to the pan and cook the onion and peppers until softened, about 5 minutes.

4 ▲ Remove the frying pan from the heat and stir in the garlic. Crumble in the bacon. Reserve the mixture in a bowl until needed.

5 ▲ Heat the remaining oil in the frying pan. Lay the potato slices in the bottom of the pan, slightly overlapping. Spoon the bacon, onion, and pepper mixture evenly over the potatoes.

6 In a small bowl, beat together the eggs, cream and salt and pepper to taste.

7 ▲ Pour the egg mixture into the frying pan. Cook over low heat until the egg is set, lifting the edge of the omelette with a knife several times to let the uncooked egg seep down.

8 Transfer the frying pan to the oven to finish cooking the omelette, 5–10 minutes longer. Serve hot or warm, cut into wedges.

Spinach and Cheese Pie

SERVES 8

3 lb (1.35 kg) fresh spinach leaves, coarse stems removed
2 tbsp olive oil
1 medium onion, finely chopped
2 tbsp chopped fresh oregano, or 1 tsp dried oregano
4 eggs
1 lb (450 g) cottage cheese
6 tbsp freshly grated Parmesan cheese
grated nutmeg
salt and pepper
12 small sheets of frozen filo pastry, thawed
2 oz (55 g) butter or margarine, melted

1 Preheat a 375°F/190°C/Gas 5 oven.

2 ▲ Stack handfuls of spinach leaves, roll them loosely and cut across the leaves into thin ribbons.

3 Heat the oil in a large saucepan. Add the onion and cook until softened, about 5 minutes.

4 Add the spinach and oregano and cook over high heat until most of liquid from the spinach evaporates, about 5 minutes, stirring frequently. Remove from the heat and let cool.

5 Break the eggs into a bowl and beat. Stir in the cottage cheese and Parmesan cheese, and season generously with nutmeg, salt and pepper. Stir in the spinach mixture.

6 ▲ Brush a 13 × 9 in (33 × 23 cm) baking dish with a little butter or margarine. Arrange half the filo sheets in the bottom of the dish to cover evenly and extend about 1 in (2.5 cm) up the sides. Brush with butter.

7 ▲ Ladle in the spinach and cheese filling. Cover with the remaining filo pastry, tucking under the edges neatly.

8 Brush the top with the remaining butter. Score the top with diamond shapes using a sharp knife.

9 Bake until the pastry is golden brown, about 30 minutes. Cut into squares and serve hot.

Spinach Moulds with Tomato Dressing

SERVES 6

1½ lb (700 g) frozen chopped spinach, thawed

1 oz (30 g) butter or margarine

3 oz (85 g) fresh breadcrumbs

salt and pepper

2 eggs

1 egg yolk

12 fl oz (350 ml) milk

3 tbsp freshly grated Parmesan cheese

fresh thyme sprigs, for garnishing

FOR THE DRESSING

5 tsp fresh lemon juice

1 tsp sugar

½ tsp whole-grain mustard

½ tsp fresh thyme leaves, or ⅛ tsp dried thyme

4 fl oz (125 ml) olive oil

3 tomatoes, peeled, seeded and diced

1 Preheat a 350°F/180°C/Gas 4 oven. Butter 6 ramekins. Place them in a shallow baking tin.

2 ▲ A handful at a time, squeeze the thawed spinach to remove as much water as possible.

3 Melt the butter or margarine in a saucepan. Stir in the spinach and cook 1 minute over a high heat, stirring.

4 ▲ Remove the pan from the heat. Stir the breadcrumbs into the spinach. Season with salt and pepper.

5 In a small bowl, beat the whole eggs with the egg yolk. Scald the milk in a small saucepan. Lightly beat it into the eggs.

6 ▲ Add the Parmesan cheese to the milk mixture and stir into the spinach mixture.

7 ▲ Spoon the mixture into the ramekins, dividing it evenly. Cover each ramekin tightly with foil.

8 ▲ Add hot water to the baking tin to come halfway up the sides of the ramekins. Bake until a knife inserted in a flan comes out clean, about 35 minutes.

9 ▲ Meanwhile, for the dressing, combine the lemon juice, sugar, mustard and thyme in a bowl. Whisk in the olive oil. Stir in the tomatoes and salt and pepper to taste.

10 To serve, unmould the flans onto individual plates. Spoon a little dressing over each flan and garnish with a sprig of fresh thyme.

~ COOK'S TIP ~

Fresh breadcrumbs are easy to make using a food processor. Remove and discard the crusts from several slices of bread. Tear the bread into smaller pieces and process.

Sweetcorn Fritters

SERVES 4

5 garlic cloves

3 eggs, beaten

3 oz (85 g) plain flour

salt and pepper

6 oz (175 g) drained canned sweetcorn,
   or frozen sweetcorn, thawed

8 fl oz (250 ml) soured cream

2 tbsp chopped fresh chives

3 tbsp corn oil

1 Preheat the grill.

2 Thread the garlic cloves onto a skewer. Grill close to the heat, turning, until charred and soft. Let cool.

3 ▼ Peel the garlic cloves. Place them in a bowl and mash with a fork. Add the eggs, flour and salt and pepper to taste and stir until well mixed. Stir in the sweetcorn. Set aside for at least 30 minutes.

4 In a small bowl, combine the soured cream and chives. Cover and refrigerate.

5 ▲ To cook the fritters, heat the oil in a frying pan. Drop in spoonfuls of the batter and fry until lightly browned on both sides, about 2 minutes, turning once. Drain on kitchen paper.

6 Serve the fritters hot with the chive dip.

Cheese and Mushroom Open Omelette

SERVES 4

2 tbsp olive oil

4 oz (115 g) small mushrooms, sliced

3 spring onions, finely chopped

6 eggs

4 oz (115 g) Cheddar cheese, grated

1 tbsp chopped fresh dill, or ¼ tsp
   dried dill

salt and pepper

1 Heat the oil in a heavy 8 in (20 cm) frying pan, preferably with an ovenproof handle. Add the mushrooms and spring onions and cook over medium heat until wilted, about 3 minutes, stirring occasionally.

2 ▲ Break the eggs into a bowl and beat to mix. Add the cheese, dill and salt and pepper to taste.

3 Preheat the grill.

4 ▼ Spread the vegetables evenly in the frying pan. Pour the egg mixture over them. Cook until the omelette is set at the edge, and the underside is golden, 5–6 minutes.

5 Place the frying pan under the grill, about 3 in (8 cm) from the heat. Grill until the top has set and is lightly browned, 3–4 minutes. Transfer to a warmed platter for serving.

Sweetcorn Fritters (top), Cheese and Mushroom Open Omelette

Baked Cheeses with Red Pepper Sauce

SERVES 4

12 oz (350 g) log of goat cheese, cut into
    12 equal slices

4 oz (115 g) dry breadcrumbs

1 tbsp chopped fresh parsley

1½ oz (45 g) Parmesan cheese, freshly
    grated

2 eggs, beaten

fresh parsley, for garnishing

FOR THE SAUCE

4 tbsp olive oil

4 garlic cloves, chopped

2 red peppers, seeded and chopped

1 tsp fresh thyme leaves

2 tsp tomato purée

salt and pepper

1 Preheat a 450°F/230°C/Gas 8 oven.

2 ▼ For the sauce, heat the olive oil in a saucepan. Add the garlic, red peppers and thyme and cook until the vegetables are soft, about 10 minutes, stirring frequently.

3 Pour the pepper mixture into a food processor or blender and purée. Return the puréed mixture to the saucepan. Stir in the tomato purée and salt and pepper to taste. Set aside.

4 ▲ Place each slice of cheese between two pieces of greaseproof paper. With the flat side of a large knife, flatten the cheese slightly.

5 ▲ In a small bowl, combine the breadcrumbs, parsley and Parmesan cheese. Pour the mixture onto a plate.

6 ▲ Dip the cheese rounds in the beaten egg, then in the breadcrumb mixture, coating well on all sides. Place on an ungreased baking tray.

7 Bake the cheese until golden, about 5 minutes. Meanwhile, gently reheat the sauce.

8 To serve, spoon some sauce on 4 heated plates. Place the baked cheese slices on top and garnish with parsley. Pass the remaining sauce.

Cheese and Dill Soufflés

SERVES 6

2 tbsp grated Parmesan cheese
2 oz (55 g) butter or margarine
1½ oz (45 g) plain flour
10 fl oz (300 ml) milk
4 oz (115 g) mature Cheddar cheese, grated
3 eggs, separated
2 tbsp chopped fresh dill
salt and pepper

1 Preheat a 400°F/200°C/Gas 6 oven. Butter 6 ramekins, and dust with the Parmesan cheese.

2 ▲ Melt the butter or margarine in a saucepan. Add the flour and cook 2 minutes, stirring. Stir in the milk. Bring to a boil, stirring constantly, and simmer until thickened, about 5 minutes. Remove from the heat and let cool about 10 minutes.

4 In a clean mixing bowl, beat the egg whites with ⅛ teaspoon salt until stiff peaks form.

6 ▲ Divide the mixture evenly between the prepared dishes. Bake until the soufflés are puffed and golden, 15–20 minutes. Serve immediately.

3 ▲ Stir the cheese, egg yolks and dill into the sauce. Season with salt and pepper. Transfer to a bowl.

5 ▲ Stir one-quarter of the egg whites into the cheese sauce mixture to lighten it. Fold in the remaining egg whites.

Asparagus, Sweetcorn and Red Pepper Quiche

SERVES 6

8 oz (225 g) fresh asparagus, woody stalks removed

1 oz (30 g) butter or margarine

1 small onion, finely chopped

1 red pepper, seeded and finely chopped

4 oz (115 g) drained canned sweetcorn, or frozen sweetcorn, thawed

2 eggs

8 fl oz (250 ml) single cream

2 oz (55 g) Cheddar cheese, grated

salt and pepper

FOR THE PASTRY

6½ oz (190 g) plain flour

½ tsp salt

4 oz (115 g) lard or vegetable fat

2–3 tbsp iced water

1 Preheat a 400°F/200°C/Gas 6 oven.

2 For the pastry, sift the flour and salt into a mixing bowl. Using a pastry blender or 2 knives, cut in the fat until the mixture resembles coarse breadcrumbs. Sprinkle in the water, 1 tablespoon at a time, tossing lightly with your fingertips or a fork until the dough forms a ball.

3 ▲ On a lightly floured surface, roll out the dough. Use it to line a 10 in (25 cm) quiche dish or loose-bottomed tart tin, easing the pastry in and being careful not to stretch it. Trim off excess pastry.

4 ▲ Line the pastry case with greaseproof paper and weigh it down with pastry weights or dried beans. Bake 10 minutes. Remove the paper and weights or beans and bake until the pastry is set and beige in colour, about 5 minutes longer. Let cool.

5 Trim the stem ends of 8 of the asparagus spears to make them 4 in (10 cm) in length. Set aside.

6 ▲ Finely chop the asparagus trimmings and any remaining spears. Place in the bottom of the case.

7 ▲ Melt the butter or margarine in a frying pan. Add the onion and red pepper and cook until softened, about 5 minutes. Stir in the sweetcorn and cook 2 minutes longer.

8 Spoon the sweetcorn mixture over the chopped asparagus.

9 ▲ In a small bowl, beat the eggs with the cream. Stir in the cheese and salt and pepper to taste. Pour into the pastry case.

10 ▲ Arrange the reserved asparagus spears like the spokes of a wheel on top of the filling.

11 Bake until the filling is set, 25–30 minutes.

~ VARIATION ~

To make individual tarts, roll out the pastry and use to line a 12-cup bun tray. For the filling, cut off and reserve the asparagus tips and chop the tender part of the stalks. Mix the asparagus and the cooked vegetables into the egg mixture with the cheese. Spoon the filling into the pastry cases and bake as directed, decreasing baking time by about 8–10 minutes.

Bread and Cheese Bake

3 tbsp butter or margarine

1 pt (625 ml) milk

3 eggs, beaten

1½ oz (45 g) Parmesan cheese, freshly grated

⅛ tsp cayenne pepper

salt and pepper

5 large, thick slices of crusty white bread

8 oz (225 g) Cheddar cheese, grated

1 Grease an oval baking dish with the butter or margarine.

2 ▼ In a bowl combine the milk, eggs, 3 tablespoons of the Parmesan cheese, the cayenne and salt and pepper to taste.

3 ▲ Cut the bread slices in half. Arrange 5 of them in the bottom of the prepared dish, overlapping the slices if necessary.

4 ▲ Sprinkle the bread with two-thirds of the Cheddar cheese. Top with the remaining bread.

5 Pour the egg mixture evenly over the bread. Press the bread down gently so that it will absorb the egg mixture. Sprinkle the top evenly with the remaining Parmesan and Cheddar cheeses. Let stand until the bread has absorbed most of the egg mixture, at least 30 minutes.

6 Preheat a 425°F/220°C/Gas 7 oven.

7 Set the baking dish in a roasting tin. Add enough boiling water to the tin to come halfway up the sides of the baking dish.

8 Place in the oven and bake 30 minutes, or until the pudding is lightly set and browned. If the pudding browns too quickly before setting, cover loosely with foil. Serve hot.

Italian Savoury Tarts

MAKES 12–18

2 eggs

3 tbsp whipping cream

3 tbsp crumbled feta cheese

salt and pepper

8 oz (225 g) tomatoes, peeled, seeded and chopped

12 fresh basil leaves, cut in thin ribbons

FOR THE PASTRY

6½ oz (190 g) plain flour

½ tsp salt

4 oz (115 g) lard or vegetable fat

2–3 tbsp iced water

1 Preheat a 400°F/200°C/Gas 6 oven.

2 For the pastry, sift the flour and salt into a mixing bowl. Using a pastry blender or 2 knives, cut in the fat until the mixture resembles coarse breadcrumbs. Sprinkle in the water, 1 tablespoon at a time, tossing lightly with your fingertips or a fork until the pastry forms a ball.

3 ▲ On a lightly floured surface, roll out the pastry thinly. With a fluted 2½ in (6 cm) pastry cutter, cut out 18 rounds. Use the rounds to line 18 cups in a small bun tray. Cut out larger rounds, if necessary, and make fewer tarts.

4 In a bowl, combine the eggs and cream and beat together. Stir in the cheese and salt and pepper to taste.

5 ▼ In a small saucepan, warm the tomatoes with the basil. Drain the tomatoes, then stir them into the egg mixture.

6 ▲ Divide the tomato mixture evenly between the pastry cases. Bake 10 minutes. Reduce the heat to 350°F/180°C/Gas 4 and bake until the filling has set and the pastry is golden brown, about 10 minutes longer. Let cool on a wire rack before serving.

BREADS, CAKES, PIES & BISCUITS

~

Both old favourites and lots of new ideas are here, for quick breads and buns, simple cakes and gateaux, fruit pies, nut pies, biscuits and delicious teatime treats.

Savoury Sweetcorn Bread

MAKES 9

2 eggs, lightly beaten
8 fl oz (250 ml) buttermilk
4 oz (115 g) plain flour
4 oz (115 g) cornmeal, or polenta
2 tsp baking powder
½ tsp salt
1 tbsp caster sugar
4 oz (115 g) Cheddar cheese, grated
8 oz (225 g) sweetcorn, fresh or frozen and thawed

1 Preheat a 400°F/200°C/Gas 6 oven. Grease a 9 in (23 cm) square baking tin.

2 Combine the eggs and buttermilk in a small bowl and whisk until well mixed. Set aside.

3 ▼ In another bowl, stir together the flour, cornmeal, baking powder, salt and sugar. Add the egg mixture and stir with a wooden spoon to combine. Stir in the cheese and sweetcorn.

4 ▲ Pour the mixture into the prepared tin. Bake until a skewer inserted in the centre comes out clean, about 25 minutes.

5 Unmould the bread onto a wire rack and let cool. Cut into 3 in (8 cm) squares for serving.

~ **VARIATION** ~

For a spicy bread, stir 2 tablespoons chopped fresh chilli peppers into the mixture with the cheese and sweetcorn.

American-Style Corn Sticks

MAKES 6

1 egg
4 fl oz (125 ml) milk
1 tbsp vegetable oil
4 oz (115 g) cornmeal, or polenta
2 oz (55 g) plain flour
2 tsp baking powder
3 tbsp caster sugar

1 Preheat a 375°F/190°C/Gas 5 oven. Grease a cast iron corn-stick mould.

2 Beat the egg in a small bowl. Stir in the milk and oil. Set aside.

3 ▼ In a mixing bowl, stir together the cornmeal or polenta, flour, baking powder and sugar. Pour in the egg mixture and stir with a wooden spoon to combine.

4 ▲ Spoon the mixture into the prepared mould. Bake until a skewer inserted in the centre of a corn stick comes out clean, about 25 minutes. Let cool in the mould on a wire rack for 10 minutes before unmoulding.

~ **COOK'S TIP** ~

You can also cook the corn sticks in éclair tins or an ordinary bun tray, reducing the cooking time by about 10 minutes.

Savoury Sweetcorn Bread (top), American-Style Corn Sticks

Courgette Loaf

MAKES 2 LOAVES

8 oz (225 g) flour
2 tsp bicarbonate of soda
1 tsp baking powder
1 tsp salt
1 tsp ground cinnamon
1 tsp grated nutmeg
3 eggs
10 oz (300 g) sugar
12 fl oz (315 ml) corn oil
1 tsp vanilla essence
about 8 oz (225 g) courgettes, grated

1 Preheat a 350°F/180°C/gas 4 oven. Grease 2 5½ × 4½ in (13 × 11 cm) tins or 1 9 × 5 in (23 × 13 cm) tin.

2 ▼ Sift the flour, bicarbonate of soda, baking powder and salt in a mixing bowl. Add the cinnamon and nutmeg, and stir to blend.

3 ▲ With an electric mixer, beat the eggs and sugar together until thick and pale. With a wooden spoon, stir in the oil, vanilla and courgettes.

4 ▲ Add the flour mixture and stir until just combined. Do not overmix the batter.

5 ▲ Pour the batter into the prepared tin. Bake in the middle of the oven until a skewer inserted in the centre comes out clean, about 1 hour for 2 smaller tins or 1¼ hours for a larger tin.

6 Let cool in the tins on a wire rack for 15 minutes, then unmould onto the wire rack to cool completely.

Sweet Potato and Raisin Bread

MAKES 1

10 oz (300 g) plain flour
2 tsp baking powder
½ tsp salt
1 tsp ground cinnamon
½ tsp grated nutmeg
1 lb (450 g) mashed cooked sweet potatoes
3½ oz (100 g) light brown sugar
4 oz (115 g) butter or margarine, melted and cooled
3 eggs, beaten
3 oz (85 g) raisins

1 ▼ Preheat a 350°F/180°C/Gas 4 oven. Grease a 9 × 5 in (23 × 13 cm) loaf tin.

2 Sift the flour, baking powder, salt, cinnamon and nutmeg into a small bowl. Set aside.

3 ▼ With an electric mixer, beat the mashed sweet potatoes with the brown sugar, butter or margarine and eggs until well mixed.

4 ▼ Add the flour mixture and the raisins. Stir with a wooden spoon until the flour is just mixed in.

5 ▲ Transfer the batter to the prepared tin. Bake until a skewer inserted in the centre comes out clean, 1–1¼ hours.

6 Let cool in the tin on a wire rack for 15 minutes, then unmould the bread from the tin onto the wire rack and let cool completely.

Banana and Nut Buns

MAKES 8

5 oz (140 g) plain flour

1½ tsp baking powder

2 oz (55 g) butter or margarine, at room temperature

6 oz (170 g) caster sugar

1 egg

1 tsp vanilla essence

about 3 medium bananas, mashed

2 oz (55 g) chopped pecans

3 fl oz (85 ml) milk

1 Preheat a 375°F/190°C/Gas 5 oven. Grease a bun tray.

2 Sift the flour and baking powder into a small bowl. Set aside.

3 ▲ With an electric mixer, cream the butter or margarine and sugar together. Add the egg and vanilla and beat until fluffy. Mix in the banana.

~ **VARIATION** ~

Use an equal quantity of walnuts instead of the pecans.

4 ▼ Add the pecans. With the mixer on low speed, beat in the flour mixture alternately with the milk.

5 Spoon the mixture into the prepared bun cups, filling them two-thirds full. Bake until golden brown and a skewer inserted into the centre of a bun comes out clean, 20–25 minutes.

6 Let cool in the tray on a wire rack for 10 minutes. To loosen, run a knife gently around each bun and unmould onto the wire rack. Let cool 10 minutes longer before serving.

Fruit and Cinnamon Buns

MAKES 8

4 oz (115 g) plain flour

1 tbsp baking powder

⅛ tsp salt

2½ oz (65 g) light brown sugar

1 egg

6 fl oz (175 ml) milk

3 tbsp vegetable oil

2 tsp ground cinnamon

5 oz (140 g) fresh or thawed frozen blueberries, or blackcurrants

1 Preheat a 375°F/190°C/Gas 5 oven. Grease a bun tray.

2 With an electric mixer, beat the first 8 ingredients together until smooth.

3 ▲ Fold in the blueberries or blackcurrants.

4 ▲ Spoon the mixture into the bun cups, filling them two-thirds full. Bake until a skewer inserted in the centre of a bun comes out clean, about 25 minutes.

5 Let cool in the bun tray on a wire rack for 10 minutes, then unmould the buns onto the wire rack and allow to cool completely.

Banana and Nut Buns (top), Fruit and Cinnamon Buns

Buttermilk Scones

MAKES 10

8 oz (225 g) plain flour
1 tsp baking powder
½ tsp bicarbonate of soda
1 tsp salt
2 oz (55 g) butter or margarine, chilled
6 fl oz (175 ml) buttermilk

~ COOK'S TIP ~

If time is short, drop heaped tablespoonfuls of the biscuit mixture onto the baking tray without kneading or cutting it out.

1 Preheat a 425°F/220°C/Gas 7 oven.

2 ▼ Sift the flour, baking powder, bicarbonate of soda and salt into a mixing bowl. Cut in the butter or margarine with a fork until the mixture resembles coarse breadcrumbs.

3 ▲ Add the buttermilk and mix until well combined to a soft dough.

4 ▲ Turn the dough onto a lightly floured board and knead 30 seconds.

5 ▲ Roll out the dough to ½ in (1 cm) thickness. Use a floured 2½ in (6 cm) pastry cutter to cut out rounds.

6 Transfer the rounds to a baking tray and bake until golden brown, 10–12 minutes. Serve hot.

Savoury Parmesan Puddings

Makes 6

8 tbsp freshly grated Parmesan cheese
4 oz (115 g) plain flour
¼ tsp salt
2 eggs
8 fl oz (250 ml) milk
1 tbsp butter or margarine, melted

1 ▼ Preheat a 450°F/230°C/Gas 8 oven. Grease 6 individual baking tins. Sprinkle each pan with 1 tablespoon of the grated Parmesan. Alternatively, you can use ramekins, in which case, heat them on a baking tray in the oven, then grease and sprinkle with Parmesan just before filling.

2 Sift the flour and salt into a small bowl. Set aside.

3 ▲ In a mixing bowl, beat together the eggs, milk and butter or margarine. Add the flour mixture and stir until smoothly blended.

4 ▼ Divide the batter evenly among the containers, filling each one about half full. Bake for 15 minutes, then sprinkle the tops of the puddings with the remaining grated Parmesan cheese. Reduce the heat to 350°F/ 180°C/Gas 4 and continue baking until the puddings are firm and golden brown, 20–25 minutes.

5 ▲ Remove the puddings from the oven. To unmould, run a thin knife around the inside of each tin to loosen them. Gently ease out, then transfer to a wire rack to cool.

Traditional Chocolate Cake

SERVES 10

4 oz (115 g) plain chocolate
9 fl oz (275 ml) milk
7 oz (200 g) light brown sugar
1 egg yolk
9 oz (260 g) plain flour
1 tsp bicarbonate of soda
½ tsp salt
5 oz (140 g) butter or margarine, at room temperature
9 oz (260 g) caster sugar
3 eggs
1 tsp vanilla essence
FOR THE ICING
8 oz (225 g) plain chocolate
¼ tsp salt
6 fl oz (175 ml) soured cream

1 Preheat a 350°F/180°C/Gas 4 oven. Line 2 × 8–9 in (20–23 cm) round cake tins with greaseproof paper.

2 ▲ In a heatproof bowl set over a pan of simmering water, or in a double boiler, combine the chocolate, one-third of the milk, the brown sugar and egg yolk. Cook, stirring, until smooth and thickened. Let cool.

3 ▲ Sift the flour, bicarbonate of soda and salt into a bowl. Set aside.

4 ▲ With an electric mixer, cream the butter or margarine with the caster sugar until light and fluffy. Beat in the whole eggs, one at a time. Mix in the vanilla.

5 On low speed, beat the flour mixture into the butter mixture alternately with the remaining milk, beginning and ending with flour.

6 ▲ Pour in the chocolate mixture and mix until just combined.

7 Divide the cake mixture evenly between the cake tins. Bake until a skewer inserted in the centre comes out clean, 35–40 minutes.

8 Let cool in the tins on wire racks for 10 minutes, then unmould the cakes from the tins onto the wire racks and let cool completely.

9 ▲ For the icing, melt the chocolate in a heatproof bowl set over a pan of hot, not boiling, water, or in the top of a double boiler. Remove the bowl from the heat and stir in the salt and soured cream. Let cool slightly.

10 ▲ Set 1 cake layer on a serving plate and spread with one-third of the icing. Place the second cake layer on top. Spread the remaining icing all over the top and sides of the cake, swirling it to make a decorative finish.

Coconut Cake

SERVES 10

6 oz (175 g) icing sugar

4 oz (115 g) plain flour

12 fl oz (375 ml) egg whites (about 12)

1½ tsp cream of tartar

8 oz (225 g) caster sugar

¼ tsp salt

2 tsp almond essence

3½ oz (100 g) desiccated coconut

FOR THE ICING

2 egg whites

4 oz (115 g) caster sugar

¼ tsp salt

2 tbsp cold water

2 tsp almond essence

7 oz (200 g) desiccated coconut, toasted

3 ▲ Continue beating until stiff and glossy. Swiftly beat in the reserved 2 tablespoons of sugar, with the salt and almond essence.

6 ▲ As soon as the cake is done, turn the tin upside down and suspend its funnel over the neck of a funnel or bottle. Let cool, about 1 hour.

1 ▲ Preheat a 350°F/180°C/Gas 4 oven. Sift the icing sugar and flour into a bowl. Set aside.

2 With an electric mixer, beat the egg whites with the cream of tartar on medium speed until very thick. Turn the mixer to high speed and beat in the caster sugar, 2 tablespoons at a time, reserving 2 tablespoons.

4 ▲ One heaped teaspoon at a time, sprinkle the flour mixture over the meringue, quickly folding until just combined. Fold in the desiccated coconut in 2 batches.

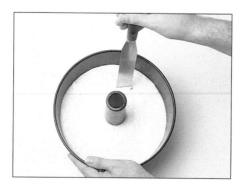

5 ▲ Transfer the cake mixture to an ungreased 10 in (25 cm) non-stick tube tin, and cut gently through the mixture with a metal spatula. Bake until the top of the cake springs back when touched lightly, 30–35 minutes.

7 ▲ For the icing, combine the egg whites, sugar, salt and water in a heatproof bowl. Beat with an electric mixer until blended. Set the bowl over a pan of boiling water and continue beating on medium speed until the icing is stiff, about 3 minutes. Remove the pan from the heat and stir in the almond essence.

8 ▲ Unmould the cake onto a serving plate. Spread the icing gently over the top and sides of the cake. Sprinkle with the toasted coconut.

Carrot Cake

SERVES 10

1 lb (450 g) caster sugar

8 fl oz (250 ml) vegetable oil

4 eggs

about 8 oz (225 g) carrots, finely grated

8 oz (225 g) plain flour

1½ tsp bicarbonate of soda

1½ tsp baking powder

1 tsp ground allspice

1 tsp ground cinnamon

FOR THE ICING

8 oz (225 g) icing sugar

8 oz (225 g) cream cheese, at room temperature

2 oz (55 g) butter or margarine, at room temperature

2 tsp vanilla essence

6 oz (175 g) chopped walnuts or pecans

1 Preheat a 375°F/190°C/Gas 5 oven.

2 Butter and flour 2 × 9 in (23 cm) round cake tins.

3 ▲ In a mixing bowl, combine the caster sugar, vegetable oil, eggs, and carrots. Beat for 2 minutes.

4 Sift the dry ingredients into another bowl. Add in 4 equal batches to the carrot mixture, mixing well after each addition.

5 ▲ Divide the cake mixture evenly between the prepared cake tins. Bake until a skewer inserted in the centre of the cake comes out clean, 35–45 minutes.

6 Let cool in the tins on wire racks for 10 minutes, then unmould the cakes from the tins onto the wire racks and let cool completely.

7 For the icing, combine everything but the nuts in a bowl and beat until smooth.

8 ▲ To assemble, set 1 cake layer on a serving plate and spread with one-third of the icing. Place the second cake layer on top. Spread the remaining icing all over the top and sides of the cake, swirling it to make a decorative finish. Sprinkle the nuts around the top edge.

Apple and Pear Frying-Pan Cake

SERVES 6

1 apple, peeled, cored and thinly sliced
1 pear, peeled, cored and thinly sliced
2 oz (55 g) chopped walnuts
1 tsp ground cinnamon
1 tsp grated nutmeg
3 eggs
3 oz (85 g) plain flour
1 oz (30 g) light brown sugar
6 fl oz (175 ml) milk
1 tsp vanilla essence
2 oz (55 g) butter or margarine
icing sugar, for sprinkling

1 ▲ Preheat a 375°F/190°C/Gas 5 oven. In a mixing bowl, toss together the apple and pear slices, walnuts, cinnamon and nutmeg. Set aside.

2 ▲ With an electric mixer, beat together the eggs, flour, brown sugar, milk and vanilla.

3 ▼ Melt the butter or margarine in a 9–10 in (23–25 cm) ovenproof frying pan (preferably cast iron) over medium heat. Add the apple mixture. Cook until lightly caramelized, about 5 minutes, stirring occasionally.

4 ▲ Pour the mixture over the fruit and nuts. Transfer the frying pan to the oven and bake until the cake is puffy and pulling away from the sides of the pan, about 30 minutes.

5 Sprinkle the cake lightly with icing sugar and serve hot.

Ginger Cake with Spiced Whipped Cream

SERVES 9

6 oz (170 g) plain flour

2 tsp baking powder

½ tsp salt

2 tsp ground ginger

2 tsp ground cinnamon

1 tsp ground cloves

¼ tsp grated nutmeg

2 eggs

8 oz (225 g) caster sugar

8 fl oz (250 ml) whipping cream

1 tsp vanilla essence

icing sugar, for sprinkling

FOR THE SPICED WHIPPED CREAM

6 fl oz (175 ml) whipping cream

1 tsp icing sugar

¼ tsp ground cinnamon

¼ tsp ground ginger

⅛ tsp grated nutmeg

1 Preheat a 350°F/180°C/Gas 4 oven. Grease a 9 in (23 cm) square baking tin.

2 Sift the flour, baking powder, salt and spices into a bowl. Set aside.

3 ▲ With an electric mixer, beat the eggs on high speed until very thick, about 5 minutes. Gradually beat in the caster sugar.

4 ▲ With the mixer on low speed, beat in the flour mixture alternately with the cream, beginning and ending with the flour. Stir in the vanilla.

5 ▲ Pour the cake mixture into the tin and bake until the top springs back when touched lightly, 35–40 minutes. Let cool in the tin on a wire rack for 10 minutes.

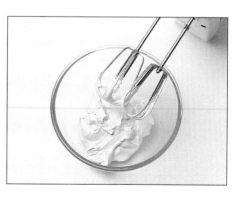

6 ▲ Meanwhile, to make the spiced whipped cream, combine the ingredients in a bowl and whip until the cream will hold soft peaks.

7 Sprinkle icing sugar over the hot cake, cut in 9 squares, and serve with spiced whipped cream.

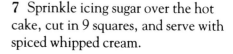

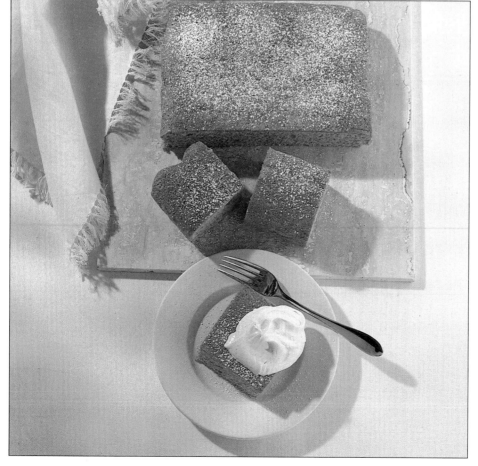

Madeira Cake

SERVES 12

8 oz (225 g) plain flour
1 tsp baking powder
8 oz (225 g) butter or margarine, at room temperature
8 oz (225 g) caster sugar
grated rind of 1 lemon
1 tsp vanilla essence
4 eggs

1 Preheat a 325°F/170°C/Gas 3 oven. Grease a 9 × 5 in (23 × 13 cm) loaf tin.

2 Sift the flour and baking powder into a small bowl. Set aside.

3 ▲ With an electric mixer, cream the butter or margarine, adding the sugar 2 tablespoons at a time, until light and fluffy. Stir in the lemon rind and vanilla.

4 ▲ Add the eggs one at a time, beating for 1 minute after each addition.

5 ▼ Add the flour mixture and stir until just combined.

6 ▲ Pour the cake mixture into the tin and tap lightly. Bake until a metal skewer inserted in the centre comes out clean, about 1¼ hours.

7 Let cool in the tin on a wire rack for 10 minutes, then unmould the cake from the tin onto the wire rack and let cool completely.

Apple Cake

SERVES 10

1½ lb (700 g) apples, peeled, cored and quartered
1 lb 2 oz (500 g) caster sugar
1 tbsp water
12 oz (350 g) plain flour
1¾ tsp bicarbonate of soda
1 tsp ground cinnamon
1 tsp ground cloves
6 oz (170 g) raisins
5 oz (140 g) chopped walnuts
8 oz (225 g) butter or margarine, at room temperature
1 tsp vanilla essence

FOR THE ICING

4 oz (115 g) icing sugar
¼ tsp vanilla essence
2–3 tbsp milk

1 ▲ Combine the apples, 2 oz (55 g) of the sugar and the water in a medium saucepan and bring to a boil. Simmer 25 minutes, stirring occasionally with a wooden spoon to break up any lumps. Let cool.

~ COOK'S TIP ~

Be sure to grease the cake tin generously and allow this cake to become completely cold before unmoulding it.

2 ▲ Preheat a 325°F/170°C/Gas 3 oven. Butter and flour a 3–3½ pt (1.75–2 litre) tube tin.

3 Sift the flour, bicarbonate of soda and spices into a mixing bowl. Remove 2 tablespoons of the mixture to a bowl and toss with the raisins and all but 1 oz (30 g) of the walnuts.

4 ▲ With an electric mixer, cream the butter or margarine and remaining sugar together until light and fluffy. Fold in the apple mixture gently with a wooden spoon.

5 ▲ Fold the flour mixture into the apple mixture. Stir in the vanilla and the raisin and walnut mixture.

6 Pour the cake mixture into the prepared tin. Bake until a skewer inserted in the centre comes out clean, about 1½ hours.

7 Let cool in the tin on a wire rack for 20 minutes, then unmould the cake from the tin onto the wire rack and let cool completely.

8 ▲ For the icing, put the sugar in a bowl and stir in the vanilla and 1 tablespoon of the milk. Add the remaining milk, teaspoon by teaspoon, until the icing is smooth and has a thick pouring consistency.

9 ▲ Transfer the cooled cake to a serving plate and drizzle the icing on top. Sprinkle with the remaining nuts. Let the cake stand for 2 hours before slicing, so the icing can set.

Pumpkin Pie

SERVES 8

about 9 oz (250 g) puréed pumpkin

16 fl oz (450 ml) single cream

4½ oz (135 g) light brown sugar

¼ tsp salt

1 tsp ground cinnamon

½ tsp ground ginger

¼ tsp ground cloves

⅛ tsp grated nutmeg

2 eggs

FOR THE PASTRY

5½ oz (165 g) plain flour

½ tsp salt

4 oz (115 g) lard or vegetable fat

2–3 tbsp iced water

1½ oz (45 g) pecans, chopped

1 Preheat a 425°F/220°C/Gas 7 oven.

2 ▲ For the pastry, sift the flour and salt into a mixing bowl. Using a pastry blender, cut in the fat until the mixture resembles coarse breadcrumbs. Sprinkle in the water, 1 tablespoon at a time, tossing lightly with a fork until the mixture forms a ball.

3 ▲ On a lightly floured surface, roll out the pastry to ¼ in (5 mm) thickness. Use it to line a 9 in (23 cm) pie tin. Ease the pastry in without stretching it. Trim off the excess.

4 ▲ If you like, use the pastry trimmings to make a decorative rope edge. Cut in strips and twist together in pairs. Dampen the rim of the pastry case and press on the rope edge. Or, with your thumbs, make a fluted edge. Sprinkle the chopped pecans over the bottom of the case.

5 With a whisk or an electric mixer on medium speed, beat together the puréed pumpkin, cream, brown sugar, salt, spices and eggs.

6 Pour the pumpkin mixture into the pastry case. Bake 10 minutes, then reduce the heat to 350°F/180°C/Gas 4 and continue baking until the filling is set, about 45 minutes. Let the pie cool in the tin, set on a wire rack.

Maple Syrup and Pecan Pie

SERVES 8

3 eggs, beaten
3½ oz (100 g) dark brown sugar
5 fl oz (150 ml) golden syrup
3 fl oz (85 ml) maple syrup
½ tsp vanilla essence
⅛ tsp salt
4 oz (115 g) pecan halves
FOR THE PASTRY
5½ oz (165 g) plain flour
½ tsp salt
1 tsp ground cinnamon
4 oz (115 g) lard or vegetable fat
2–3 tbsp iced water

1 Preheat a 425°F/220°C/Gas 7 oven.

2 For the pastry, sift the flour, salt and cinnamon into a mixing bowl. Using a pastry blender, cut in the fat until the mixture resembles coarse breadcrumbs. Sprinkle in the water, 1 tablespoon at a time, tossing lightly with your fingertips or a fork until the mixture forms a ball.

3 On a lightly floured surface, roll out the pastry to a circle 15 in (38 cm) in diameter. Use it to line a 9 in (23 cm) pie tin, easing in the pastry and being careful not to stretch it.

4 ▲ With your thumbs, make a fluted edge. Using a fork, prick the bottom and sides of the pastry case all over. Bake until lightly browned, 10–15 minutes. Let cool in the tin.

5 ▼ Reduce the oven temperature to 350°F/180°C/Gas 4. In a bowl, stir together the eggs, sugar, syrups, vanilla and salt until well mixed.

6 ▲ Sprinkle the pecans evenly over the bottom of the baked pastry case. Pour in the egg mixture. Bake until the filling is set and the pastry is golden brown, about 40 minutes. Let cool in the tin, set on a wire rack.

Traditional Apple Pie

SERVES 8

about 2 lb (900 g) tart eating apples, such as Granny Smith, peeled, cored and sliced
1 tbsp fresh lemon juice
1 tsp vanilla essence
4 oz (115 g) caster sugar
½ tsp ground cinnamon
1½ oz (45 g) butter or margarine
1 egg yolk
2 tsp whipping cream
FOR THE PASTRY
8 oz (225 g) plain flour
1 tsp salt
6 oz (170 g) lard or vegetable fat
4–5 tbsp iced water
1 tbsp quick-cooking tapioca

1 Preheat a 450°F/230°C/Gas 8 oven.

2 For the pastry, sift the flour and salt into a bowl. Using a pastry blender, cut in the fat until the mixture resembles coarse breadcrumbs.

3 ▲ Sprinkle in the water, 1 tablespoon at a time, tossing lightly with your fingertips or with a fork until the pastry forms a ball.

4 ▲ Divide the pastry in half and shape each half into a ball. On a lightly floured surface, roll out one of the balls to a circle about 12 in (30 cm) in diameter.

5 ▲ Use it to line a 9 in (23 cm) pie tin, easing the dough in and being careful not to stretch it. Trim off the excess pastry and use the trimmings for decorating. Sprinkle the tapioca over the bottom of the pie shell.

6 ▲ Roll out the remaining pastry to ⅛ in (3 mm) thickness. With a sharp knife, cut out 8 large leaf-shapes. Cut the trimmings into small leaf shapes. Score the leaves with the back of the knife to mark veins.

7 ▲ In a bowl, toss the apples with the lemon juice, vanilla, sugar and cinnamon. Fill the pastry case with the apple mixture and dot with the butter or margarine.

8 ▲ Arrange the large pastry leaves in a decorative pattern on top. Decorate the edge with small leaves.

9 ▲ Mix together the egg yolk and cream and brush over the leaves to glaze them.

10 Bake 10 minutes, then reduce the heat to 350°F/180°C/Gas 4 and continue baking until the pastry is golden brown, 35–45 minutes. Let the pie cool in the tin, set on a wire rack.

Rich Chocolate Pie

SERVES 8

3 oz (85 g) plain chocolate
2 oz (55 g) butter or margarine
3 tbsp golden syrup
3 eggs, beaten
5 oz (140 g) caster sugar
1 tsp vanilla essence
4 oz (115 g) milk chocolate
16 fl oz (500 ml) whipping cream
FOR THE PASTRY
5½ oz (165 g) plain flour
½ tsp salt
4 oz (115 g) lard or vegetable fat
2–3 tbsp iced water

1 Preheat a 425°F/220°C/Gas 7 oven.

2 For the pastry, sift the flour and salt into a mixing bowl. Using a pastry blender, cut in the fat until the mixture resembles coarse breadcrumbs. Sprinkle in the water, 1 tablespoon at a time. Toss lightly with a fork until the pastry forms a ball.

3 On a lightly floured surface, roll out the pastry. Use to line an 8 or 9 in (20 or 23 cm) pie tin, easing in the pastry and being careful not to stretch it. Make a fluted edge.

4 Using a fork, prick the bottom and sides of the pastry case all over. Bake until lightly browned, 10–15 minutes. Let cool, in the tin, on a wire rack.

5 ▲ In a heatproof bowl set over a pan of simmering water, or in a double boiler, melt the plain chocolate, the butter or margarine and golden syrup. Remove the bowl from the heat and stir in the eggs, sugar and vanilla.

6 Reduce the oven temperature to 350°F/180°C/Gas 4. Pour the chocolate mixture into the case. Bake until the filling is set, 35–40 minutes. Let cool in the tin, set on a rack.

7 ▲ For the decoration, use the heat of your hands to soften the chocolate bar slightly. Draw the blade of a swivel-headed vegetable peeler along the side of the chocolate bar to shave off short, wide curls. Chill the chocolate curls until needed.

8 Before serving, lightly whip the cream until soft peaks form. Using a rubber spatula, spread the cream over the surface of the chocolate filling. Decorate with the chocolate curls.

Creamy Banana Pie

SERVES 6

7 oz (200 g) ginger biscuits, finely crushed

2½ oz (70 g) butter or margarine, melted

½ tsp grated nutmeg or ground cinnamon

6 oz (175 g) ripe bananas, mashed

12 oz (350 g) cream cheese, at room temperature

2 fl oz (65 ml) thick plain yogurt or soured cream

3 tbsp dark rum or 1 tsp vanilla essence

FOR THE TOPPING

8 fl oz (250 ml) whipping cream

3–4 bananas

1 Preheat a 375°F/190°C/Gas 5 oven.

2 ▲ In a mixing bowl, combine the crushed biscuits, butter or margarine and spice. Mix thoroughly with a wooden spoon.

3 ▲ Press the biscuit mixture into a 9 in (23 cm) pie dish, building up thick sides with a neat edge. Bake 5 minutes. Let cool, in the dish.

4 ▼ With an electric mixer, beat the mashed bananas with the cream cheese. Fold in the yogurt or soured cream and rum or vanilla. Spread the filling in the biscuit base. Refrigerate at least 4 hours or overnight.

5 ▲ For the topping, whip the cream until soft peaks form. Spread on the pie filling. Slice the bananas and arrange on top in a decorative pattern.

Lime Meringue Pie

SERVES 8

3 egg yolks
12 fl oz (350 ml) sweetened condensed milk
finely grated rind and juice of 4 limes
7 egg whites
⅛ tsp salt
squeeze of fresh lemon juice
4 oz (115 g) sugar
½ tsp vanilla essence
FOR THE PASTRY
5½ oz (165 g) plain flour
½ tsp salt
4 oz (115 g) lard or vegetable fat
2–3 tbsp iced water

1 Preheat a 425°F/220°C/Gas 7 oven.

2 ▲ For the pastry, sift the flour and salt into a mixing bowl. Using a pastry blender or 2 knives, cut in the fat until the mixture resembles coarse breadcrumbs. Sprinkle in the water, 1 tablespoon at a time, tossing lightly with a fork until the mixture forms a ball.

~ COOK'S TIP ~

When beating egg whites with an electric mixer, start slowly, and increase speed after they become frothy. Turn the bowl constantly.

3 ▲ On a lightly floured surface, roll out the pastry. Use it to line a 9 in (23 cm) pie tin, easing in the pastry. Make a fluted edge.

4 Using a fork, prick the bottom and sides of the pastry case all over. Bake until lightly browned, 10–15 minutes. Let cool, in the tin, on a wire rack. Reduce oven temperature to 350°F/180°C/Gas 4.

5 ▲ With an electric mixer on high speed, beat the yolks and condensed milk. Stir in the lime rind and juice.

6 ▲ In another clean bowl, beat 3 of the egg whites until stiff. Fold into the lime mixture.

7 ▲ Spread the lime filling in the pastry case. Bake 10 minutes.

8 ▲ Meanwhile, beat the remaining egg whites with the salt and lemon juice until soft peaks form. Beat in the sugar, 1 tablespoon at a time, until stiff peaks form. Add the vanilla.

9 ▲ Remove the pie from the oven. Using a metal spatula, spread the meringue over the lime filling, making a swirled design and covering the surface completely.

10 Bake until the meringue is lightly browned and the pastry is golden brown, about 12 minutes longer. Let cool, in the tin, on a wire rack.

Cherry Pie

SERVES 8

2 lb (900 g) fresh Morello cherries, stoned, or 2 × 1 lb (450 g) cans or jars, drained and stoned
2½ oz (70 g) caster sugar
1 oz (30 g) plain flour
1½ tbsp fresh lemon juice
¼ tsp almond essence
1 oz (30 g) butter or margarine
FOR THE PASTRY
8 oz (225 g) plain flour
1 tsp salt
6 oz (175 g) lard or vegetable fat
4–5 tbsp iced water

1 For the pastry, sift the flour and salt into a mixing bowl. Using a pastry blender, cut in the fat until the mixture resembles coarse breadcrumbs.

2 ▲ Sprinkle in the water, 1 tablespoon at a time, tossing lightly with your fingertips or a fork until the pastry forms a ball.

3 Divide the pastry in half and shape each half into a ball. On a lightly floured surface, roll out one of the balls to a circle about 12 in (30 cm) in diameter.

4 ▲ Use it to line a 9 in (23 cm) pie tin, easing the pastry in and being careful not to stretch it. With scissors, trim off excess pastry, leaving a ½ in (1 cm) overhang around the pie rim.

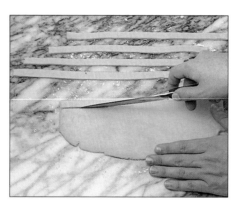

5 ▲ Roll out the remaining pastry to ⅛ in (3 mm) thickness. Cut out 11 strips ½ in (1 cm) wide.

6 ▲ In a mixing bowl, combine the cherries, sugar, flour, lemon juice and almond essence. Spoon the mixture into the pastry case and dot with the butter or margarine.

7 ▲ To make the lattice, place 5 of the pastry strips evenly across the filling. Fold every other strip back. Lay the first strip across in the opposite direction. Continue in this pattern, folding back every other strip each time you add a cross strip.

8 ▲ Trim the ends of the lattice strips even with the case overhang. Press together so that the edge rests on the pie-tin rim. With your thumbs, flute the edge. Refrigerate 15 minutes.

9 Preheat a 425°F/220°C/Gas 7 oven.

10 Bake the pie 30 minutes, covering the edge of the pastry case with foil, if necessary, to prevent over-browning. Let cool, in the tin, on a wire rack.

Ginger Biscuits

MAKES 60

10 oz (300 g) plain flour
1 tsp bicarbonate of soda
1½ tsp ground ginger
¼ tsp ground cinnamon
¼ tsp ground cloves
4 oz (115 g) butter or margarine, at room temperature
12 oz (350 g) caster sugar
1 egg, beaten
4 tbsp treacle
1 tsp fresh lemon juice

1 Preheat a 325°F/170°C/Gas 3 oven. Grease 3–4 baking trays.

2 Sift the flour, bicarbonate of soda and spices into a small bowl. Set aside.

3 With an electric mixer, cream the butter or margarine and two-thirds of the sugar together.

4 ▲ Stir in the egg, treacle and lemon juice. Add the flour mixture and mix in thoroughly with a wooden spoon to make a soft dough.

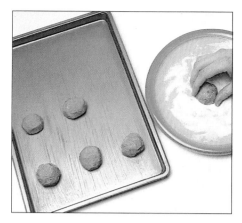

5 ▲ Shape the dough into ¾ in (2 cm) balls. Roll the balls in the remaining sugar and place about 2 in (5 cm) apart on the baking trays.

6 Bake until the biscuits are just firm to the touch, about 12 minutes. With a slotted spatula, transfer the biscuits to a wire rack and let cool.

Chocolate-Chip Oat Biscuits

MAKES 60

4 oz (115 g) plain flour
½ tsp bicarbonate of soda
¼ tsp baking powder
¼ tsp salt
4 oz (115 g) butter or margarine, at room temperature
4 oz (115 g) caster sugar
3½ oz (100 g) light brown sugar
1 egg
½ tsp vanilla essence
3 oz (85 g) rolled oats
6 oz (170 g) plain chocolate chips

1 Preheat a 350°F/180°C/Gas 4 oven. Grease 3–4 baking trays.

2 Sift the flour, bicarbonate of soda, baking powder and salt into a mixing bowl. Set aside.

3 With an electric mixer, cream the butter or margarine and sugars together. Add the egg and vanilla and beat until light and fluffy.

4 ▲ Add the flour mixture and beat on low speed until thoroughly blended. Stir in the rolled oats and chocolate chips, mixing well with a wooden spoon. The dough should be crumbly.

5 ▲ Drop heaped teaspoonfuls onto the prepared baking trays, spacing the dough about 1 in (2.5 cm) apart. Bake until just firm around the edge but still soft to the touch in the centre, about 15 minutes. With a slotted spatula, transfer the biscuits to a wire rack and let cool.

Ginger Biscuits (top), Chocolate-Chip Oat Biscuits

Traditional Sugar Biscuits

MAKES 36

12 oz (350 g) plain flour

1 tsp bicarbonate of soda

2 tsp baking powder

¼ tsp grated nutmeg

4 oz (115 g) butter or margarine, at room temperature

8 oz (225 g) caster sugar

½ tsp vanilla essence

1 egg

4 fl oz (125 ml) milk

coloured or demerara sugar, for sprinkling

1 Sift the flour, bicarbonate of soda, baking powder and nutmeg into a small bowl. Set aside.

2 ▲ With an electric mixer, cream the butter or margarine, caster sugar and vanilla together until the mixture is light and fluffy. Add the egg and beat to mix well.

3 ▲ Add the flour mixture alternately with the milk, stirring with a wooden spoon to make a soft dough. Wrap the dough in cling film and refrigerate at least 30 minutes, or overnight.

4 ▲ Preheat a 350°F/180°C/Gas 4 oven. Roll out the dough on a lightly floured surface to ⅛ in (3 mm) thickness. Cut into rounds or other shapes with biscuit cutters.

5 ▲ Transfer the biscuits to ungreased baking trays. Sprinkle each one with coloured or demerara sugar.

6 Bake until golden brown, 10–12 minutes. With a slotted spatula, transfer the biscuits to a wire rack and let cool.

Chocolate Chip Nut Biscuits

MAKES 36

4 oz (115 g) plain flour
1 tsp baking powder
¼ tsp salt
3 oz (85 g) butter or margarine, at room temperature
4 oz (115 g) caster sugar
1¾ oz (50 g) light brown sugar
1 egg
1 tsp vanilla essence
4½ oz (130 g) chocolate chips
2 oz (55 g) hazelnuts, chopped

1 ▲ Preheat a 350°F/180°C/Gas 4 oven. Grease 2–3 baking trays.

2 Sift the flour, baking powder and salt into a small bowl. Set aside.

3 ▲ With an electric mixer, cream the butter or margarine and sugars together. Beat in the egg and vanilla.

4 Add the flour mixture and beat well with the mixer on low speed.

5 ▼ Stir in the chocolate chips and half of the hazelnuts using a wooden spoon.

6 Drop teaspoonfuls of the mixture onto the prepared baking trays, to form ¾ in (2 cm) mounds. Space the biscuits 1–2 in (2–5 cm) apart.

7 ▲ Flatten each biscuit lightly with a wet fork. Sprinkle the remaining hazelnuts on top of the biscuits and press lightly into the surface.

8 Bake until golden brown, about 10–12 minutes. With a slotted spatula, transfer the biscuits to a wire rack and let cool.

Spicy Pepper Biscuits

MAKES 48

7 oz (200 g) plain flour
2 oz (55 g) cornflour
2 tsp baking powder
½ tsp ground cardamom
½ tsp ground cinnamon
½ tsp grated nutmeg
½ tsp ground ginger
½ tsp ground allspice
½ tsp salt
½ tsp freshly ground black pepper
8 oz (225 g) butter or margarine, at room temperature
3½ oz (100 g) light brown sugar
½ tsp vanilla essence
1 tsp finely grated lemon rind
2 fl oz (65 ml) whipping cream
3 oz (85 g) finely ground almonds
2 tbsp icing sugar

1 Preheat a 350°F/180°C/Gas 4 oven.

2 Sift the flour, cornflour, baking powder, spices, salt and pepper into a bowl. Set aside.

3 With an electric mixer, cream the butter or margarine and brown sugar together until light and fluffy. Beat in the vanilla and lemon rind.

4 ▲ With the mixer on low speed, add the flour mixture alternately with the cream, beginning and ending with flour. Stir in the ground almonds.

5 ▲ Shape the dough into ¾ in (2 cm) balls. Place them on ungreased baking trays about 1 in (2.5 cm) apart. Bake until the biscuits are golden brown underneath, 15–20 minutes.

6 Let the biscuits cool on the baking trays about 1 minute before transferring them to a wire rack to cool completely. Before serving, sprinkle them lightly with icing sugar.

Chocolate and Coconut Slices

MAKES 24

6 oz (175 g) digestive biscuits, crushed
2 oz (55 g) caster sugar
⅛ tsp salt
4 oz (115 g) butter or margarine, melted
3 oz (85 g) desiccated coconut
9 oz (260 g) plain chocolate chips
8 fl oz (250 ml) sweetened condensed milk
4 oz (115 g) chopped walnuts

1 Preheat a 350°F/180°C/Gas 4 oven.

2 ▼ In a bowl, combine the crushed biscuits, sugar, salt and butter or margarine. Press the mixture evenly over the bottom of an ungreased 13 × 9 in (33 × 23 cm) baking dish.

3 ▲ Sprinkle the coconut over the biscuit base, then scatter over the chocolate chips. Pour the condensed milk evenly over the chocolate. Sprinkle the walnuts on top.

4 Bake 30 minutes. Unmould onto a wire rack and let cool, preferably overnight. When cooled, cut into slices.

Spicy Pepper Biscuits (top), Chocolate and Coconut Slices

Lemon Squares

MAKES 12

8 oz (225 g) plain flour
2 oz (55 g) icing sugar
¼ tsp salt
6 oz (170 g) cold butter or margarine
1 tsp cold water
FOR THE LEMON LAYER
4 eggs
1 lb (450 g) caster sugar
1 oz (30 g) plain flour
½ tsp baking powder
1 tsp grated lemon rind
2 fl oz (65 ml) fresh lemon juice
icing sugar, for sprinkling

1 Preheat a 350°F/180°C/Gas 4 oven.

2 ▼ Sift the flour, icing sugar and salt into a mixing bowl. Using your fingertips or a pastry blender, rub or cut in the butter or margarine until the mixture resembles coarse breadcrumbs. Add the water and toss lightly with a fork until the mixture forms a ball.

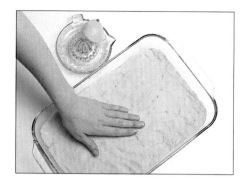

3 ▲ Press the mixture evenly into an ungreased 13 × 9 in (33 × 23 cm) baking dish. Bake until light golden brown, 15–20 minutes. Remove from oven and let cool slightly.

4 Meanwhile, with an electric mixer, beat together the eggs, caster sugar, flour, baking powder and lemon rind and juice.

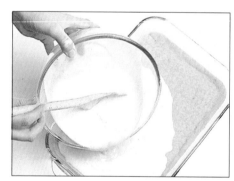

5 ▲ Pour the lemon mixture over the baked base. Return to the oven and bake 25 minutes. Let cool, in the baking dish, on a wire rack.

6 ▲ Before serving, sprinkle the top with icing sugar. Cut into squares with a sharp knife.

Hazelnut Squares

MAKES 9

2 oz (55 g) plain chocolate
2½ oz (70 g) butter or margarine
8 oz (225 g) caster sugar
2 oz (55 g) plain flour
½ tsp baking powder
2 eggs, beaten
½ tsp vanilla essence
4 oz (115 g) skinned hazelnuts, roughly chopped

1 Preheat a 350°F/180°C/Gas 4 oven. Grease an 8 in (20 cm) square baking tin.

2 ▲ In a heatproof bowl set over a pan of barely simmering water, or in a double boiler, melt the chocolate and butter or margarine. Remove the bowl from the heat.

3 ▲ Add the sugar, flour, baking powder, eggs, vanilla and half the hazelnuts to the melted mixture and stir well with a wooden spoon.

4 ▼ Pour the mixture into the prepared tin. Bake 10 minutes, then sprinkle the reserved hazelnuts over the top. Return to the oven and continue baking until firm to the touch, about 25 minutes.

5 ▲ Let cool in the tin, set on a wire rack, for 10 minutes, then unmould onto the rack and let cool completely. Cut into squares for serving.

HOT & COLD DESSERTS

~

There's always a little space left at the end of a meal for
dessert, particularly if it's rich and creamy, fruity and spiced,
crisp and nutty, icy cold, or, best of all, chocolatey.
You'll find a sweet idea here for every occasion.

Hot Spiced Bananas

SERVES 6

6 ripe bananas

7 oz (200 g) light brown sugar

8 fl oz (250 ml) unsweetened pineapple juice

4 fl oz (125 ml) dark rum

2 cinnamon sticks

12 whole cloves

1 ▼ Preheat a 350°F/180°C/Gas 4 oven. Grease a 9 in (23 cm) baking dish.

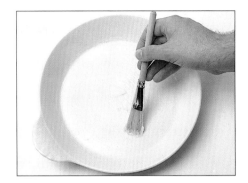

2 ▲ Peel the bananas and cut them into 1 in (2.5 cm) pieces on the diagonal. Arrange the banana pieces evenly over the bottom of the prepared baking dish.

3 ▲ In a saucepan, combine the sugar and pineapple juice. Cook over a medium heat until the sugar has dissolved, stirring occasionally.

4 Add the rum, cinnamon sticks and cloves. Bring to the boil, then remove the pan from the heat.

5 ▲ Pour the pineapple and spice mixture over the bananas. Bake until the bananas are very tender and hot, 25–30 minutes. Serve hot.

Apple and Walnut Crisp

SERVES 6

about 2 lb (900 g) tart eating apples, such as Granny Smith, peeled, cored and sliced

grated rind of ½ lemon

1 tbsp fresh lemon juice

3½ oz (100 g) light brown sugar

3 oz (85 g) plain flour

¼ tsp salt

¼ tsp grated nutmeg

½ tsp ground cardamom

½ tsp ground cinnamon

4 oz (115 g) butter or margarine, diced

2 oz (55 g) chopped walnuts

1 Preheat a 350°F/180°C/Gas 4 oven. Grease a 9–10 in (23–25 cm) oval gratin dish or shallow baking dish.

2 ▲ Toss the apples with the lemon rind and juice. Arrange them evenly in the bottom of the prepared dish.

3 In a mixing bowl, combine the brown sugar, flour, salt, nutmeg, cardamom and cinnamon. With 2 knives, or a pastry blender, cut in the butter or margarine until the mixture resembles coarse breadcrumbs. Mix in the walnuts.

4 ▼ With a spoon, sprinkle the walnut and spice mixture evenly over the apples. Cover with foil and bake for 30 minutes.

5 ▲ Remove the foil and continue baking until the apples are tender and the topping is crisp, about 30 minutes longer. Serve warm.

Baked Apples with Caramel Sauce

Serves 6

3 Granny Smith apples, cored but not peeled

3 Red Delicious apples, cored but not peeled

5 oz (140 g) light brown sugar

6 fl oz (175 ml) water

½ tsp grated nutmeg

¼ tsp freshly ground black pepper

1½ oz (45 g) walnut pieces

1½ oz (45 g) sultanas

2 oz (55 g) butter or margarine, diced

FOR THE CARAMEL SAUCE

½ oz (15 g) butter or margarine

4 fl oz (125 ml) whipping cream

1   Preheat a 375°F/190°C/Gas 5 oven. Grease a baking tin just large enough to hold the apples.

2 ▲   With a small knife, cut at an angle to enlarge the core opening at the stem-end of each apple to about 1 in (2.5 cm) in diameter. (The opening should resemble a funnel in shape.)

~ **VARIATION** ~

Use a mixture of firm red and gold pears instead of the apples, preparing them the same way. Cook for 10 minutes longer.

3 ▲   Arrange the apples in the prepared tin, stem-end up.

4 ▲   In a small saucepan, combine the brown sugar, water, nutmeg and pepper. Bring the mixture to the boil, stirring. Boil for 6 minutes.

5 ▲   Mix together the walnuts and sultanas. Spoon some of the walnut-sultana mixture into the opening in each apple.

6 ▲   Top each apple with some of the diced butter or margarine.

7 ▲   Spoon the brown sugar sauce over and around the apples. Bake, basting occasionally with the sauce, until the apples are just tender, about 50 minutes. Transfer the apples to a serving dish, reserving the brown sugar sauce in the baking tin. Keep the apples warm.

8 ▲   For the caramel sauce, mix the butter or margarine, cream and reserved brown sugar sauce in a saucepan. Bring to the boil, stirring occasionally, and simmer until thickened, about 2 minutes. Let the sauce cool slightly before serving.

Upside-Down Pear Pudding

Serves 8

2 oz (55 g) plain flour

1 tsp baking powder

¼ tsp salt

7 oz (200 g) plain chocolate

4 oz (115 g) butter or margarine

2 eggs

4 oz (115 g) caster sugar

½ tsp vanilla essence

1 tbsp strong black coffee

1½ oz (45 g) plain chocolate chips

3 oz (85 g) walnuts, chopped

1½ lb (700 g) ripe pears, or 2 × 14 oz (400 g) cans pear quarters, drained

1 Preheat a 375°F/190°C/Gas 5 oven. Grease a 9 in (23 cm) round non-stick baking dish.

2 Sift the flour, baking powder and salt into a small bowl. Set aside.

3 In a heatproof bowl set over a pan of simmering water, or in a double boiler, melt the chocolate and butter or margarine. Remove the bowl from the heat and let cool slightly.

4 ▲ Beat the eggs, sugar, vanilla and coffee into the melted chocolate mixture. Stir in the flour mixture, chocolate chips and walnuts.

5 ▲ If using fresh pears, peel, quarter and core them. Arrange the pear quarters in the prepared baking dish, with the rounded ends against the side of the dish. Pour the pudding mixture evenly over the pears.

6 Bake 1 hour, covering with foil after 30 minutes. Let cool 15 minutes, then hold an upturned plate tightly over the top of the baking dish, invert and unmould. Serve hot.

Baked Pears with Ginger

Serves 6

6 large firm pears, peeled, cored and sliced lengthwise

3 fl oz (85 ml) honey

2 oz (55 g) light brown sugar

1 tbsp finely grated fresh root ginger

4 fl oz (125 ml) whipping cream

~ **VARIATION** ~

Substitute firm (even under-ripe) peaches for the pears. To peel, dip the peaches in boiling water for about a minute, then slip off the skins. Cook as for pears.

1 ▼ Preheat a 400°F/200°C/Gas 6 oven. Butter a 10 in (25 cm) oval gratin dish or shallow baking dish. Fan the pear slices in a spiral design in the bottom of the baking dish.

2 ▲ In a small bowl, mix together the honey, brown sugar, grated root ginger and cream. Pour this mixture over the pears.

3 Bake until the pears are tender and the top is lightly golden, about 30 minutes. Serve hot.

Upside-Down Pear Pudding (top), Baked Pears with Ginger

Summer Berry Pudding

SERVES 8

8 oz (225 g) plain flour

2 tsp baking powder

½ tsp salt

4 oz (115 g) butter or margarine, at room temperature

5 oz (140 g) caster sugar

1 egg

½ tsp vanilla essence

6 fl oz (175 ml) milk

10 oz (300 g) blueberries, or blackcurrants

whipped cream, for serving

FOR THE TOPPING

3½ oz (100 g) light brown sugar

2 oz (55 g) plain flour

½ tsp salt

½ tsp ground allspice

2 oz (55 g) butter or margarine

2 tsp milk

1 tsp vanilla essence

1 Preheat a 375°F/190°C/Gas 5 oven. Grease a 9 in (23 cm) round gratin dish or shallow baking dish.

2 Sift the flour, baking powder and salt into a small bowl. Set aside.

3 ▲ With an electric mixer, or using a wooden spoon, cream together the butter or margarine and caster sugar. Beat in the egg and vanilla. Add the flour mixture alternately with the milk, beginning and ending with the flour.

4 ▲ Pour the mixture into the prepared dish. Sprinkle the fruit evenly over the mixture.

5 ▲ For the topping, combine the brown sugar, flour, salt and allspice in a bowl. With a pastry blender, cut in the butter until the mixture resembles coarse breadcrumbs.

6 ▲ Mix together the milk and vanilla. Drizzle over the flour mixture and toss lightly with a fork to mix.

7 Sprinkle the topping over the fruit. Bake until a skewer inserted in the centre comes out clean, about 45 minutes. Serve warm, with whipped cream, if wished.

Peach Cobbler

SERVES 6

about 3 lb (1.35 kg) peaches, peeled and sliced
3 tbsp caster sugar
2 tbsp peach brandy
1 tbsp fresh lemon juice
1 tbsp cornflour
FOR THE TOPPING
4 oz (115 g) plain flour
1½ tsp baking powder
¼ tsp salt
1½ oz (45 g) finely ground almonds
2 oz (55 g) caster sugar
2 oz (55 g) butter or margarine
3 fl oz (85 ml) milk
¼ tsp almond essence

1 Preheat a 425°F/220°C/Gas 7 oven.

2 In a bowl, toss the peaches with the sugar, peach brandy, lemon juice, and cornflour.

3 Spoon the peach mixture into a 3½ pt (2 litre) baking dish.

4 ▲ For the topping, sift the flour, baking powder and salt into a mixing bowl. Stir in the ground almonds and all but 1 tablespoon of the sugar. With 2 knives, or a pastry blender, cut in the butter or margarine until the mixture resembles coarse breadcrumbs.

5 ▼ Add the milk and almond essence and stir until the topping mixture is just combined.

6 ▲ Drop the topping in spoonfuls onto the peaches. Sprinkle with the remaining tablespoon of sugar.

7 Bake until the cobbler topping is browned, 30–35 minutes. Serve hot, with ice cream, if wished.

Spiced Milk Pudding

SERVES 6

1¾ pt (1 litre) milk

1½ oz (45 g) semolina

½ tsp salt

¼ tsp ground ginger

¾ tsp ground cinnamon

2 oz (55 g) butter or margarine

8 fl oz (250 ml) treacle

2 eggs, beaten

1   Heat three-quarters of the milk in a saucepan.

2   In a heatproof bowl set over a pan of boiling water, or in a double boiler, combine the semolina, salt, ginger, cinnamon and remaining milk.

3 ▼   Pour in the heated milk, stirring to combine. Cook, stirring constantly, until smooth.

4   Reduce the heat so the water is just simmering, and cook 25 minutes, stirring frequently.

5   Preheat a 350°F/180°C/Gas 4 oven. Grease a deep 1¾ pt (1 litre) earthenware baking dish.

6 ▲   Remove the bowl from the heat. Stir in the butter or margarine and treacle until the mixture is smooth. Stir in the eggs.

7   Pour the mixture into the prepared baking dish. Bake 1 hour. Serve warm.

Lemon Sponge Pudding

SERVES 6

4 oz (115 g) plain flour

1 tsp baking powder

¼ + ⅛ tsp salt

4 oz (115 g) butter or margarine, at room temperature

10 oz (300 g) caster sugar

finely grated rind and juice of 4 large lemons

4 eggs, separated

10 fl oz (300 ml) milk

1   Preheat a 350°F/180°C/Gas 4 oven. Butter a 10 in (25 cm) baking dish.

2   Sift the flour, baking powder and ¼ teaspoon salt into a small bowl. Set aside.

3 ▼   With an electric mixer, beat together the butter or margarine, sugar and lemon rind. Beat in the egg yolks, one at a time. Mix in the flour mixture alternately with the milk and lemon juice (reserving a squeeze of juice), beginning and ending with the flour.

4 ▲   In a clean bowl, beat the egg whites with the ⅛ teaspoon salt and squeeze of lemon juice until stiff peaks form. Fold into the lemon mixture.

5   Pour into the prepared baking dish. Bake until golden brown, 40–45 minutes. Serve hot.

Spiced Milk Pudding (top), Lemon Sponge Pudding

Bread Pudding with Whiskey Sauce

SERVES 8

about 6 oz (170 g) stale French bread, in ¾ in (2 cm) cubes

16 fl oz (450 ml) milk

2 eggs

8 oz (225 g) caster sugar

1 tbsp vanilla essence

½ tsp ground cinnamon

¼ tsp grated nutmeg

2 oz (55 g) butter or margarine, melted and cooled slightly

3 oz (85 g) raisins

FOR THE SAUCE

2 egg yolks

4 oz (115 g) butter or margarine

8 oz (225 g) sugar

3 fl oz (85 ml) bourbon or Irish whiskey

1 ▲ Preheat a 350°F/180°C/Gas 4 oven. Grease an 8 in (20 cm) baking dish.

2 ▲ Put the bread cubes in a bowl with the milk and squeeze the bread with your hands until well saturated.

3 ▲ With an electric mixer on high speed, beat the eggs with the sugar until pale and thick. Stir in the vanilla, cinnamon, nutmeg, butter or margarine and raisins.

4 ▲ Add the soaked bread cube mixture and stir well to mix. Let stand 10 minutes.

5 ▲ Transfer the mixture to the prepared baking dish. Bake until firm and a knife inserted in the middle comes out clean, 45–50 minutes. Let it cool slightly in the dish, set on a wire rack.

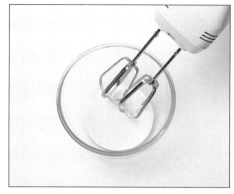

6 ▲ Meanwhile, make the sauce. With an electric mixer, beat the egg yolks until thick and pale.

7 ▲ Melt the butter or margarine and sugar in a saucepan. Pour the butter and sugar mixture over the egg yolks, beating constantly, until well thickened. Stir in the whiskey.

8 Serve the warm pudding from its baking dish. Pass the hot whiskey sauce separately.

~ COOK'S TIP ~

It is important to allow enough time for the egg mixture to soak the bread thoroughly; otherwise the bread cubes will float on top, leaving a layer of custard on the bottom when the dish is cooked.

Rich Chocolate Pudding

SERVES 6

3 oz (85 g) plain flour

2 tsp baking powder

⅛ tsp salt

2 oz (55 g) butter or margarine, at room temperature

1 oz (30 g) plain chocolate

4 oz (115 g) caster sugar

3 fl oz (85 ml) milk

¼ tsp vanilla essence

whipped cream, for serving

FOR THE TOPPING

2 tbsp instant coffee

10 fl oz (315 ml) hot water

3½ oz (100 g) dark brown sugar

2½ oz (70 g) caster sugar

2 tbsp unsweetened cocoa powder

1 Preheat a 350°F/180°C/Gas 4 oven. Grease a 9 in (23 cm) square non-stick baking tin.

2 Sift the flour, baking powder and salt into a small bowl. Set aside.

3 In a heatproof bowl set over a pan of simmering water, or in a double boiler, melt the butter or margarine, chocolate and caster sugar, stirring occasionally. Remove the bowl from the heat.

4 ▲ Add the flour mixture and stir well. Stir in the milk and vanilla.

5 ▲ Pour the mixture into the prepared baking tin.

6 For the topping, dissolve the coffee in the water. Let cool.

7 ▲ Mix together the sugars and cocoa powder and sprinkle over the pudding mixture.

8 ▲ Pour the coffee evenly over the surface. Bake 40 minutes. Serve immediately with whipped cream.

Individual Chocolate Soufflés

SERVES 6

2½ oz (70 g) caster sugar

2 oz (55 g) plus 1 tbsp unsweetened cocoa powder

3 fl oz (85 ml) cold water

6 egg whites

icing sugar, for dusting

1 Preheat a 375°F/190°C/Gas 5 oven. Lightly butter 6 individual soufflé dishes or ramekins. Mix together 1 tablespoon of the sugar and 1 tablespoon of cocoa powder. Sprinkle this mixture over the bottom and sides of the dishes and shake out any excess.

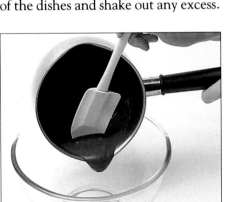

2 ▲ In a saucepan, combine the remaining cocoa powder and the cold water. Bring to the boil over medium heat, whisking constantly. Pour into a mixing bowl.

3 ▲ With an electric mixer, beat the egg whites until soft peaks form. Add the remaining sugar and continue beating until the peaks are stiff.

4 ▼ Add one-quarter of the egg whites to the chocolate mixture and stir well to combine. Add the remaining egg whites and fold gently but thoroughly, until no streaks of white are visible.

5 ▲ Divide the chocolate mixture between the prepared dishes, filling them to the top. Smooth the surface with a metal spatula. Run your thumb around the rim of each dish so the mixture will not stick when rising.

6 Bake until well risen and set, 14–16 minutes. Dust with icing sugar and serve immediately.

Fruit Kebabs with Mango and Yoghurt Sauce

SERVES 4

½ pineapple, peeled, cored and cubed

2 kiwi fruit, peeled and cubed

5 oz (140 g) strawberries, hulled and cut in half lengthwise, if large

½ mango, peeled, stoned and cubed

FOR THE SAUCE

4 fl oz (125 ml) fresh mango purée, from 1–1½ peeled and stoned mangoes

4 fl oz (125 ml) thick plain yoghurt

1 tsp sugar

⅛ tsp vanilla essence

1 tbsp finely shredded fresh mint leaves

1 To make the sauce, beat together the mango purée, yoghurt, sugar and vanilla with an electric mixer.

2 ▼ Stir in the mint. Cover the sauce and refrigerate until required.

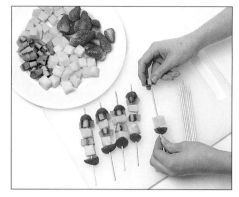

3 ▲ Thread the fruit onto 12 × 6 in (15 cm) wooden skewers, alternating the pineapple, kiwi fruit, strawberries and mango cubes.

4 Arrange the kebabs on a large serving platter with the mango and yoghurt sauce in the centre.

Tropical Fruits in Cinnamon Syrup

SERVES 6

1 lb (450 g) caster sugar

1 cinnamon stick

1 large or 2 medium papayas (about 1½ lb/700 g), peeled, seeded and cut lengthwise into thin pieces

1 large or 2 medium mangoes (about 1½ lb/700 g), peeled, stoned and cut lengthwise into thin pieces

1 large or 2 small starfruit (about 8 oz/ 225 g), thinly sliced

1 Sprinkle one-third of the sugar over the bottom of a large saucepan. Add the cinnamon stick and half the papaya, mango and starfruit pieces.

2 ▼ Sprinkle half of the remaining sugar over the fruit pieces in the pan. Add the remaining fruit and sprinkle with the remaining sugar.

3 Cover the pan and cook the fruit over medium-low heat until the sugar dissolves completely, 35–45 minutes. Shake the pan occasionally, but do not stir or the fruit will collapse.

4 ▲ Uncover the pan and simmer until the fruit begins to appear translucent, about 10 minutes. Remove the pan from the heat and let stand to cool. Remove the cinnamon stick.

5 Transfer the fruit and syrup to a bowl, cover and refrigerate overnight.

~ **COOK'S TIP** ~

Starfruit is sometimes called carambola.

Fruit Kebabs with Mango and Yoghurt Sauce (top), Tropical Fruits in Cinnamon Syrup

Rice Pudding with Soft Fruit Sauce

SERVES 6

12 oz (350 g) short-grain rice
11 fl oz (335 ml) milk
⅛ tsp salt
3½ oz (100 g) light brown sugar
1 tsp vanilla essence
2 eggs, beaten
grated rind of 1 lemon
1 tsp fresh lemon juice
1 oz (30 g) butter or margarine
FOR THE SAUCE
5 oz (140 g) strawberries, hulled and quartered
4 oz (115 g) raspberries
4 oz (115 g) caster sugar
grated rind of 1 lemon

1 Preheat a 325°F/170°C/Gas 3 oven. Grease a deep 3½ pt (2 litre) baking dish.

2 ▼ Bring a saucepan of water to the boil. Add the rice and boil 5 minutes. Drain. Transfer the rice to the prepared baking dish.

3 In a bowl, combine the milk, salt, brown sugar, vanilla, eggs and lemon rind and juice. Pour this mixture over the rice and stir well.

4 ▲ Dot the surface of the rice mixture with the butter or margarine. Bake until the rice is cooked and creamy, about 50 minutes.

5 ▲ Meanwhile, for the sauce, combine the fruit and sugar in a small saucepan. Stir over low heat until the sugar dissolves completely and the fruit is becoming pulpy. Transfer to a bowl and stir in the lemon rind. Refrigerate until required.

6 ▲ Remove the rice pudding from the oven. Let cool completely, and serve with the berry sauce.

Surprise Fruit Baskets

SERVES 6

4 large or 8 small sheets of frozen filo pastry, thawed
2½ oz (70 g) butter or margarine, melted
8 fl oz (250 ml) whipping cream
3 tbsp strawberry jam
1 tbsp Cointreau or other orange flavoured liqueur
4 oz (115 g) seedless black grapes, halved
4 oz (115 g) seedless white grapes, halved
5 oz (140 g) fresh pineapple, cubed, or drained canned pineapple chunks
4 oz (115 g) raspberries
2 tbsp icing sugar
6 sprigs of fresh mint, for garnishing

1 Preheat a 350°F/180°C/Gas 4 oven. Grease 6 cups of a bun tray.

2 ▲ Stack the filo sheets and cut with a sharp knife or scissors into 24 × 4½ in (11 cm) squares.

3 ▲ Lay 4 squares of pastry in each of the 6 greased cups. Press the pastry firmly into the cups, rotating slightly to make star-shaped baskets.

4 ▼ Brush the pastry baskets lightly with butter or margarine. Bake until the pastry is crisp and golden, 5–7 minutes. Let cool on a wire rack.

5 In a bowl, lightly whip the cream until soft peaks form. Gently fold the strawberry jam and Cointreau into the cream.

6 ▲ Just before serving, spoon a little of the cream mixture into each pastry basket. Top with the fruit. Sprinkle with icing sugar and decorate each basket with a small sprig of mint.

Strawberry Shortcake

SERVES 6

1 lb (450 g) strawberries, hulled and halved or quartered, depending on size
3 tbsp icing sugar
8 fl oz (250 ml) whipping cream
mint leaves, for garnishing
FOR THE SHORTCAKE
8 oz (225 g) plain flour
3 oz (85 g) caster sugar
1 tbsp baking powder
½ tsp salt
8 fl oz (250 ml) whipping cream

1 Preheat a 400°F/200°C/Gas 6 oven. Lightly grease a baking tray.

2 ▲ For the shortcake, sift the flour into a mixing bowl. Add 2 oz (55 g) of the caster sugar, the baking powder and salt. Stir well.

3 ▲ Gradually add the cream, tossing lightly with a fork until the mixture forms clumps.

4 ▲ Gather the clumps together, but do not knead the dough. Shape the dough into a 6 in (15 cm) log. Cut into 6 slices and place them on the prepared baking tray.

5 ▲ Sprinkle with the remaining 1 oz (30 g) caster sugar. Bake until light golden brown, about 15 minutes. Let cool on a wire rack.

6 ▲ Meanwhile, combine one-quarter of the strawberries with the icing sugar. Mash with a fork. Stir in the remaining strawberries. Let stand 1 hour at room temperature.

7 ▲ In a bowl, whip the cream until soft peaks form.

8 ▲ To serve, slice each shortcake in half horizontally using a serrated knife. Put the bottom halves on individual dessert plates. Top each half with some of the whipped cream. Divide the strawberries among the 6 shortcakes. Replace the tops and garnish with mint. Serve with the remaining whipped cream.

~ COOK'S TIP ~

For best results when whipping cream, refrigerate the bowl and beaters until thoroughly chilled. If using an electric mixer, increase speed gradually, and turn the bowl while beating to incorporate as much air as possible.

Italian Trifles

SERVES 4

8 oz (225 g) mascarpone cheese

1½ tbsp caster sugar

2 eggs, at room temperature, separated

⅛ tsp salt

squeeze of fresh lemon juice

4 fl oz (125 ml) very strong cold black
  coffee

2 tbsp coffee liqueur

4 oz (115 g) biscuits, macaroons or
  Madeira cake, coarsely crumbled

2 tbsp cocoa powder, sifted

~ COOK'S TIP ~

Buying very fresh eggs from a
reputable producer is especially
important when using them raw.

---

1 With an electric mixer, beat the
cheese, sugar and egg yolks together
until blended and creamy.

2 ▲ In a clean mixing bowl, beat the
egg whites with the salt and lemon
juice until stiff peaks form. Fold into
the cheese mixture.

3 In a small bowl, combine the coffee
and liqueur.

4 ▲ Divide half the crushed biscuits
among 4 stemmed glasses. Drizzle over
1–1½ tablespoons of the liqueur
mixture. Top the moistened biscuits
with half the mascarpone mixture.
Layer the remaining biscuits, coffee
mixture and mascarpone mixture in
the same way.

5 Cover and refrigerate the desserts
for 1–2 hours. Sprinkle with the sifted
cocoa powder before serving.

White Chocolate Mousse

SERVES 8

9 oz (250 g) white chocolate

3 fl oz (85 ml) milk

12 fl oz (350 ml) whipping cream

1 tsp vanilla essence

3 egg whites, at room temperature

⅛ tsp salt

squeeze of fresh lemon juice

chocolate covered coffee beans, for
  decoration (optional)

---

1 In a heatproof bowl set over a pan
of barely simmering water, or in a
double boiler, melt the chocolate.

2 Scald the milk in a small saucepan.
Remove the bowl of chocolate from
the heat and whisk in the warm milk
until smooth. Let cool.

3 In a mixing bowl, whip the cream
with the vanilla until soft peaks form.
Refrigerate until needed.

4 ▲ Using an electric mixer and a
clean bowl, beat the egg whites with
the salt and lemon juice until stiff
peaks form (do not overbeat or the
mousse will be grainy). Fold into the
chocolate mixture.

5 ▲ Gently fold the chocolate and
egg white mixture into the vanilla
flavoured whipped cream.

6 Transfer to a pretty serving bowl or
individual stemmed glasses. Cover
and refrigerate at least 1 hour.
Sprinkle with chocolate covered
coffee beans before serving, if wished.

Italian Trifles (top), White Chocolate Mousse

Chocolate Cheesecake

SERVES 12

1 lb (450 g) plain chocolate, broken into pieces

4 oz (115 g) caster sugar

2 tsp vanilla essence

4 eggs

1½ lb (700 g) cream cheese, at room temperature

2–3 tbsp icing sugar, for decoration

FOR THE BASE

4 oz (115 g) digestive biscuits, crushed

2½ oz (70 g) butter or margarine, melted

2 tbsp grated plain chocolate

1 oz (30 g) caster sugar

1 ▲ Preheat a 325°F/170°C/Gas 3 oven. Grease a 9–10 in (23–25 cm) springform tin and line the bottom with greased greaseproof paper.

~ **VARIATION** ~

For an all-chocolate cheesecake, substitute an equal quantity of finely crushed chocolate wafers for the digestive biscuits when preparing the base. For a special topping, pipe whipped cream around the top of the cheesecake and sprinkle with icing sugar.

2 ▲ For the base, mix together the crushed biscuits, melted butter or margarine, grated chocolate and sugar. Pat evenly over the bottom and up the sides of the prepared tin. (The base will be thin.)

3 ▲ In a heatproof bowl set over a pan of barely simmering water, or in a double boiler, melt the chocolate with the caster sugar. Remove the bowl from the heat and stir in the vanilla. Let cool briefly.

4 ▲ In another bowl, beat together the eggs and cream cheese until smooth and well combined. Gently stir in the cooled chocolate mixture until completely blended.

5 ▲ Pour the chocolate filling into the biscuit base. Bake until the filling is set, 45 minutes.

6 ▲ Let cool, in the tin, on a wire rack. Refrigerate at least 12 hours.

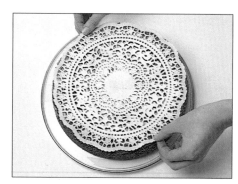

7 ▲ Remove the side of the tin and transfer the cheesecake to a serving plate. To decorate, lay a paper doily on the surface of the cake and sift the icing sugar evenly over the doily. With two hands, carefully lift off the doily.

Coffee Ice Cream Sandwiches

MAKES 8

4 oz (115 g) butter or margarine, at room temperature
2 oz (55 g) caster sugar
4 oz (115 g) plain flour
2 tbsp instant coffee
icing sugar, for sprinkling
16 fl oz (450 ml) coffee ice cream
2 tbsp cocoa powder, for sprinkling

1 Lightly grease 2–3 baking trays.

2 With an electric mixer or wooden spoon, beat the butter or margarine until soft. Beat in the caster sugar.

3 ▲ Add the flour and coffee and mix by hand to form an evenly blended dough. Wrap in a plastic bag and refrigerate at least 1 hour.

4 Lightly sprinkle the work surface with icing sugar. Knead the dough on the sugared surface for a few minutes to soften it slightly.

5 ▼ Using a rolling pin dusted with icing sugar, roll out the dough to ⅛ in (3 mm) thickness. With a 2½ in (6 cm) fluted pastry cutter, cut out 16 rounds. Transfer the rounds to the prepared baking trays. Refrigerate for at least 30 minutes.

6 Preheat a 300°F/150°C/Gas 2 oven. Bake the biscuits until they are lightly golden, about 30 minutes. Let them cool and firm up before removing them from the trays to a wire rack to cool completely.

7 Remove the ice cream from the freezer and let soften 10 minutes at room temperature.

8 ▲ With a metal spatula, spread the ice cream evenly on the flat side of eight of the biscuits, leaving the edges clear. Top with the remaining biscuits, flat-side down.

9 Arrange the ice cream sandwiches on a baking tray. Cover and freeze at least 1 hour, longer if a firmer sandwich is desired. Sift the cocoa powder over the tops before serving.

INDEX

~